AC[...]

First and foremost, [...] friend and confidant – my wife, [...] I've pursued and realized my dreams, doing what I love to do the most – Stand-Up Comedy. Thank you for suggesting I put my pen where my mouth is, to put down the stories from the road and the lessons learned along the way. Jill, thank you for taking my hand, and holding on for this life, our journey; a journey that's been rich with laughter and fun; a journey made stronger with shared tears. If you look up at the tote board, it reads LOVE.

Of course I want to thank my children, *my girls*. The saying goes, "You can't pick your parents." As truthful as that is, I want you to know how thankful and honored I am for being chosen to be your dad! My hope is that maybe, just maybe, one day you'll hand this book to *your* children and fully understand the depths of the words written and proudly say, "Your grandfather loved me very much."

I'd like to thank my friend from the Midwest, Sally Lentz, for taking on the great task of following my voice to places other people could never venture; for hearing what I said, then mindfully editing to ensure it never lost my voice. You make me a better person. It takes a certain type of circus person to capture the comedic rhythm. It was an honor, years ago, to have lunch with you in Cleveland. *When the student is ready, the teacher arrives!*

I want to thank Adam Poe (no relation to Edgar) for his ability to see the overview of where I was going and guiding each chapter to a safe, organized landing each time – even when I missed the runway! Your keen sense of how a story should flow and follow through let me know there was always a net under me as I let fly – and I thank you for that.

Finally, there is no way I would be, or could ever have been, the Stand-Up Comedian I am today... without an audience. So it is that I would like to offer my heartfelt appreciation to my followers and fans. Thank you for paying your hard-earned money to come out to see me perform and hopefully forget your problems (even if it's only for a short time) while we share our laughter. My sincere desire is to send you home feeling lighter than when you came in. Your support and acknowledgment through the years – from small clubs to large theaters, heartwarming charity events to tremendous fundraisers – is what makes me a better performer and a better human being.

Cover Art & Web Design:
Thanks to Gordon Feinberg at B Likable Interactive for his hard work and creativity.

LIKABLE

CHAPTERS

INTRODUCTION

I don't consider myself a smart person. I read the paper and I watch television, listening to all the people who I assume are smart, or at least smarter than me. Yet there are many times I wish I were smarter. I fear in the back of my mind that one day I'm going to be "outed;" that I'll overhear someone say, "Oh, that Bobby... he's a nice guy, but what a dumb son-of-a-bitch!"

Or when one of my kids asks me to help with their homework, there'll be this too-long pause as I bend over the notebook and stutter trying to explain the matter; one, or both of them, will roll their eyes and tell me, "Dad, it's cool. I can figure it out."

My wife thinks I'm a smart guy and that feels good. Even so, there's a part of me that wants to sit her down and tell her the truth: "I'm not a smart guy!"

I have this vast amount of knowledge floating around in my head; bits and pieces of subjects unrelated to each other that I hope will one day suddenly connect into "smart." So while I wait for these molecules to miraculously match up, I've taken a step back and looked at what I have learned while making America laugh. I've spent decades as a stand-up comic, on the road working comedy clubs, theaters, and casinos across the country from one coast to the other, from big cities to one-street-light towns and you know what? I've learned a few things along the way. There are universal truths out there. I may not be that smart, but that doesn't mean I don't observe and understand a universal truth when I hear one. I play well with others!

You don't have to be exceptionally smart to take the best of what you learn from experience and then use what's proven to work. I've lived and learned and experienced *a lot*. By writing this book, I want to share what I've found to be true and what works for me – and what I think will work for you.

Don't get me wrong; my purpose is not to preach to

anyone. Except, perhaps, to one of my daughters, but she doesn't want to hear it anyway (I'm still amazed when she readily listens to people who are practically strangers, but not her own personal private life tutor – me, James Bond.)

What I have learned during my time on this planet is that life's little (and big) lessons can be an exercise in fun. They're funny and easier to grasp if I'm *enjoying* the experience. This book is my invitation to you to *enjoy yourself.* Join me as I share how I celebrate the triumphs of life and handle its disappointments.

Maybe you'll get mad, perhaps even shed a tear, or you might even want to busta move – but hopefully you'll laugh along the way. In the end, I promise you will finish this book with at least a smile on your face.

I stand on a stage and show people themselves; I strip away all the pretenses and b.s. to get to the core – which is getting people to see themselves as they really are and recognize that we're sharing the planet with a lot of different folks. I'm only the mirror. If you think about it, I'm really performing a service. Just think of all the money everyone saves on their professional therapy bills! When I can get an audience to laugh, and laugh hard – at themselves – there's nothing better. I love it!

So buckle up, sit back and enjoy the ride. Like the sign posted at the amusement park says, "Please keep your hands and feet inside the vehicle at all times."

Get comfortable, turn off your phone, stop texting, and let me share with you how I discovered that life truly IS a journey and not a destination.

PROLOGUE

"Daddy, is it OK if I go over to Mira's house to play?" My oldest daughter, who was then nine, asks as we turn into our driveway.

In typical "dumb dad" mode, I start in. "Mira? Which one's Mira? Where does she live? Do her parents live there too? Does she have a dog? Does the dog bite? Does the dog have bad breath? Is she going to pay you for being her friend for the day?"

Laughing, she tells me, "Oh, Daddy, you know Mira. She lives across the street!"

Stopping the car, I turn to face my daughter, my mouth and eyes wide open with surprise, "Well, surrrrre, that Mira! OK, but don't forget, look both ways crossing the one-way street."

With that, she gives me a peck on the cheek, hops out of the car and runs down the driveway.

My wife, Jill, sitting in the seat next to me, slaps my arm and asks, "Why do you tell her those dumb things?"

Rubbing my arm, I answer, "What dumb things?"

"You know, what you just said about looking both ways before crossing a one-way street and all the other things you're always telling her," she says, getting out of the car and walking toward our backdoor.

Walking behind her, it takes a few minutes for me to react before I strongly announce, "Those are not dumb sayings! Those are 'words of wisdom!'"

"Bobby, words of wisdom are things like, 'Life is not a dress rehearsal; Live life to its fullest; Look before you leap.' You know, things that aren't...."

"Aren't what?" I ask.

"Well... aren't silly. Her little head is full of your silly sayings!"

"Whoa! I tell her these things 'cause I love her. My sayings are important. They're a result of the lessons I've learned – from encounters I've had, places I've been, and people I've met. Granted, maybe they're not all Hallmark greeting cards, but I sure as hell wish someone would have shared a couple of those 'silly sayings' with me. Because life gets a little tricky, and this is good stuff I'm telling her; stuff that hopefully makes her journey a little easier than mine has been. Hell, I hope she does more than learn something from them; I hope she shares them with all her friends and they share them with their parents!"

Jill interrupts me, "Well, if they're *that* important, *that* special, *that* necessary and that *wise*... why then don't you just write them down and put them into a book?"

DING! DING! DING! I am proud to present... *On the Inside: Witisms and Wisdomisms* (See, once in a while, I actually do listen to what she says).

Chapter 1
WE ALL BEGIN THIS RACE AT THE START
—Melissa Etheridge

They say (and I don't know who *they* are) that to understand where you're going is to know where you came from. So let's start at the beginning – where I came from. This way I can show you where my "I'm not good enough" baggage was packed and then carried by my strong "I'll fight against injustice anywhere" attitude – both of which have equally contributed to and shaped my journey.

I am a product of Queens! Oh, not my parents – they were your regular, run-of-the-mill, married male and female – living in Queens, New York, where I was born, and where I spent my formative years.

People tend to think of New York City as one big place. Actually, New York City is made up of five boroughs, and each borough has its own reputation and style. First, there's my borough: *Queens* – in the shadow of Manhattan; poor, working class, struggling people hoping to make it out to Long Island or Manhattan (or New Jersey if they have lower expectations – got the picture?). *Manhattan* is the tits – expensive, classy, upscale, the center of culture, always on the go, the "king city" of the world – if you want to buy baboon snot on a Ritz cracker at three in the morning, you can get it in Manhattan! *Brooklyn* is over there, with its thick "Toity-Toid Street and Toid Avenue" accent that you've heard in every movie ever made about New York. Did you know if Brooklyn were a city, it would be the fourth largest in the country? *The Bronx* – culturally diverse, carry a weapon with you and don't drive through it at night. Yet Yankee Stadium calls it home. Once, when I was a kid, they had bat day in the Bronx – only once – twenty-eight concussions in one day! You don't give Puerto Ricans wood (it's a New York joke!). *Staten Island* – Italian; growing up we called it *Gilligan's Island*, with more fountains in front of houses than anywhere this side of Florence! It's also a place where no one ever takes down their Christmas lights – it's a practicality thing. Why take them down? Christmas is only twelve months away. The toll to get out to Staten Island is $18 – which explains the small number of casual visitors.

THERE ARE EVENTS IN OUR LIVES THAT HAVE A PROFOUND EFFECT ON OUR PSYCHE. NO MATTER HOW SMALL OR LARGE THESE EVENTS APPEAR TO OTHERS.

Growing up in Queens, we lived in what were called the "garden apartments," although I never saw a plant of any kind – just cement and trees where dogs would take their turn. The buildings were old army barracks converted into public housing for poor people like us. It wouldn't be until much later that I realized the garden apartments were the training bra for the struggling classes – everyone growing to develop their middle-class bosom! It was genetic bouillabaisse; poor people from all over trying to get a start in New York. The funny thing about being poor is you don't know any different. We were all happy and we were all the same – poor! If one kid was fortunate enough to get a basketball, it was like we all received this treasure. What's the point of having something if you can't share it with others? That wouldn't be any fun! Poor was poor. It had no color; it was generic.

Of course, there were schmucks, pricks, perverts, and evil people who lived at our garden apartments, too, but you're going to have those wherever you live. It was only later, when I grew up a little, ventured out and met other people, that I saw how poor we really were.

Another commonality in the "gardens" was that all the kids were latchkey kids. We'd come home from school and let ourselves into our apartment. But if you forgot your key, or worse, lost your key, you had to either wait it out at a friend's (who *had* their key) or wait out in the cold or rain or snow or any combination of those three, until one of your parents came home. Boy, those were the days I really wished we had a *house* so I could crawl through the window!

9

But getting locked out on nice days wasn't a big deal to any of us. We'd entertain ourselves by playing out in the streets, which is what we'd do anyway after school and on the weekends. We'd play outside until it was time to come home for dinner, eat and then go right back out until it got dark. We were taught to watch our backs and also look out for each other. We'd play games like Hide & Go Seek, with the boundaries being Brooklyn to the north and Manhattan to the south. We could also go into the Bronx, but no one ever wanted to go there, so our parents didn't have to worry about it.

Some kids never did make it back home. I was at an airport recently and ran into one of the kids from the old neighborhood.

"Joey, what the hell ever happened to you?"

"I got lost," he told me, "but then it all worked out for the best. I started a better life!"

I told him I had no idea why his parents never really looked for him that hard, but I guess in their defense, he *was* nine years old at the time – a New York City nine – so realistically, he *knew* how to take care of himself!

We also had a lot of flat-leavers in my neighborhood – people who would leave you flat so they could go with other people who had better stuff to play with... and you weren't invited! Flat-leavers were usually Indian Givers, too. They'd give you something to keep and then take it back by saying, "I just lent it to you." To which we'd call out, "Same to you and many more, hope you die in Creedmoor!" or some other equally brilliant response. Creedmoor was the state mental hospital behind our garden apartments. The first time I saw *One Flew Over the Cuckoo's Nest,* I thought it was a home movie. There were always breakouts at Creedmoor and sometimes murders. Not exactly Mister Rogers' neighborhood!

It was always special when the Good Humor truck stopped by our neighborhood. Ice cream trucks would drive through all the poor neighborhoods, only to be followed by the impromptu choir of, "Mom, can I have fifteen cents for a pop?" And if there was another kid around, "My treat" always followed. Life was good, we had ice cream, we were free to run the neighborhood; we had parents who loved us, who put food in our bellies, a roof over our head and if we got out of line... made certain we got beat!

My father would take us on road trips to Massachusetts, usually during the summer, to visit our paternal grandparents and my oldest brother Tommy, who was sent to live with my grandparents when he was eight years old. Yes, to answer your question, I did think it was strange that my parents sent their first-born to be raised by my grandparents in another state – but later on, when I finally worked up the courage to ask, I was told by my parents that they were having problems at the time and it was best for him to live there. That was all the information I ever received. I sometimes wonder how being sent away affected my brother. Was this the first pebble that grew to become the chip he eventually carried around on his shoulder his whole life? Who knows?

I do know that when we would go visit Tommy, I would look at his room and think, *Wow! He doesn't have to share it with anyone else! How lucky is he?* He also got to live in this huge house, with separate floors and a room where they all sat down for dinner together and ate really good food. My grandparents' house had a big winding driveway with land behind it, not to mention a dog, a barn, a chicken coop and lots of love. Wow, what a dream!

Growing up in Massachusetts, Tommy excelled at almost everything he did – he was a sports star, voted Most Popular in his yearbook and worked at the local beach club (which meant he was allowed to use the club at certain times and charge hamburgers against his pay!) I was proud of him... Hell, *I wanted to be him!* I felt lucky that my parents let me spend the summers with him in Massachusetts rather than on the steamy sidewalks of New York where the smell of urine permeated the air.

One summer, we drove to visit him at a special place called Camp Jabberwocky on Martha's Vineyard (near Cape Cod), where he worked as the head counselor. The ride was five hours just to get to the ferry that took you to the camp. The long ride made me grumpy, but I didn't care because I was going to see my big brother – *my* hero! When we arrived at the camp, there were a lot of people there with Down syndrome or cerebral palsy. Many were in wheelchairs or walking around with crutches. Some were even in iron leg braces or wearing helmets. Standing tall in the middle of all this was Tommy – *my big brother* – confidently barking out directions to all the counselors.

When Tommy saw me, he didn't give me a smile or a hug, he gave me a directive: "Bobby, we're short of hands! Give Ronny a piggyback ride down to the lake. Just follow everyone!" Now, mind you, Ronny was an older man with cerebral palsy and I was a twelve-year-old boy whose maybe sixty pounds soaking wet. But – by God – if Tommy wants me to carry Ronny to the lake, then I'm carrying Ronny to the lake!

The minute I get Ronny on my back, his arms and legs start flailing all over the place. At the same time, I immediately start dripping in sweat, which makes me terrified I'm going to drop him. The whole time I'm walking to the lake I'm screaming on the inside – *He's too heavy! Someone please help me!* But I didn't want to let Tommy down... and I definitely didn't want to let Ronny down! To this day, I still don't know how I managed to successfully carry Ronny all by myself, but I did! And when Tommy sees Ronny and me standing by the lake, he calls out, "Good job, Bobby!" *That's all I needed to hear.*

DEVIATING FROM THE NORMS OF SOCIAL BEHAVIOUR IN A WAY REGARDED AS BAD

Even if you had (senior moment) an Ozzie and Harriet childhood, or came from a totally dysfunctional family – and let's face it, isn't *every* family dysfunctional on some level? (Exhibit 1, Ricky Nelson.) The fact is, your family is what molds your character for better or worse. Either because of who they are and those particular relationships OR in spite ofthem!

Trust me on this. If you look up the word dysfunction in the dictionary, you'll find a 3 x 5 glossy color photo of *my* family staring right back at you! In front are my two crazy but loving brothers (always following a different drummer), and sitting right beside them is my sister – my lovable, caring, sister – who, I might add, came to terms much later in life with the fact that being a "tomboy" (as my mother used to say) was, as they both secretly suspected, indeed more than just a phase. My poor sister would believe anything my mother told her! To save on electricity, my mother did what any poor mother would do to try and cut expenses – she told all of us, "If you leave the refrigerator door open longer than it takes to grab something out, the whole thing will blow up!" She didn't have the time or energy to explain the nuances of household budgeting to us, so she simply instilled fear. Of course, her warning didn't last too long for my brothers and me. We'd stand and stare into our open refrigerator for as long as it took to conjure up our desired food, but that warning went deep with my sister. Years later, her husband at the time, Kenny, had to explain to her, "That's impossible," after she screamed at him, "Close that refrigerator door right NOW! You've had it open too long! The whole thing is gonna blow up!"

Next to my sister is me, Bobby, the survivalist, always searching and wanting more, but not sure where to find it. There we all are, sitting directly in front of old mom and dad. Ah, Mom, who can trace her lineage back to a broken washing machine on a porch in Louisiana, now homesteading in a borough of New York City. And Dad, standing as silent as he was in real life – cardboard cutouts had more personality! He was a so stiff, Chinese tourists used to stop by our house just to take pictures with him! Dad – a good man, a New England man.

It's one thing to be dysfunctional, but as you know, we also had that additional character-building block – poverty. And when I say poverty, I don't mean POOR – we were "Po'!" Poor people would come to our house just to feel better about themselves. We were so poor that other poor people would ask each other, "Why don't we stop by the poorhouse this

13

afternoon and pay a visit? You know, the Collins' house."
Remember that saying, "If you keep this up, you're going to
drive us to the poorhouse!" I always thought people meant my
house!

The only clothes my brothers and I ever had were hand-
me-downs... *from my sister!* I know I'm repeating myself here,
but I want to make it clear when I tell you I didn't grow up
rich, I'm not talking middle-class, I'm talking poor, *really poor*
– several levels down on the poor scale. Poor with a capital P!
As Mitt Romney would say, the lower 47%. We had to work
ourselves up to poor just to start even!

Growing up, I often heard my mom say, "Oh, don't
worry, I'll make it fit. It just needs a hem! She said this so
many times that for years I thought my brothers' names were
Hem! She made us pants – *from curtains*! And then she tried to
convince us these were the next big style! But you know what?
We *believed* her. She was our mom and we knew she would
never lie to us... at least, we thought she wouldn't. I know her
heart was in the right place, but come on! We looked like
window treatments!

My father worked as an underwriter for a small
insurance company *way downtown* in Manhattan, near Battery
Park. It took him three hours a day to travel back and forth to
work; first on a bus, then subways, then later, after we moved
to Long Island, on the Long Island Railroad. And that's only if
the trains were running on time or running at all. His commute
for work was fifteen hours a week, times fifty-one weeks per
year (one week for vacation). That's thirty-one and three-
quarters days a year just traveling! That's a rolling prison! I
never saw my father in the morning, and at night, he'd come
home for dinner around six-thirty or seven; eat, read and then
right into bed. The next day, it started all over again. Try to
relate this concept to your children in an effort to help them
understand the strong parental drive to provide for your
family... then stick a needle in your eye!

My mother, as I've said, was from Louisiana,
specifically a Shreveport household of twelve – nine girls and
three boys. Hence, the names of my brothers and sisters are

mainly southern names: Roy, Dolores, Bobby and, my father's one and only stake, George Jr. However, his namesake was only on paper because George was *always* known as Tommy.

My mom ran away from home and met my father at a USO center during World War II. When she met him – the only child from a New England home – in her mind, she'd hit "pay dirt."

As it turned out, she had the dirt part right. Because, during the years we lived in Queens, my mom also needed to work – as a waitress in Manhattan, at the Gaiety Deli. While she had no education and no marketable skills, she did have a heart as big as the Grand Canyon and shared her unbridled love and compassion not only with her family, but also with friends and an occasional stranger or two. It was my mom who taught all of us about service to others.

One time I bought one of those "trying to look cool" mock turtleneck, chick-magnet shirts, with some money I'd saved up from my part-time job. I bought the shirt and put it away to wear to this special event that was coming up on Friday night – actually, I was hoping it would help me get lucky! When Friday night rolled around, I went to go put it on, but couldn't find it. I asked my mom where it was and she told me, "I gave it to this poor man down the street who really needed it. His shirt had holes in it and you have so many shirts." She gave it to him without any hesitation and with no expectation of receiving anything in return. What I learned that day was the epitome of *true giving*. Oh, and there was a smidge of learning forgiveness too, since she also inadvertently dashed any dream I might have had about getting lucky that night!

I was fairly young when I started noticing that people liked me and other kids wanted to hang out with me. But along with that, I picked up that some people felt sorry for me; were looking down at me. I wore my brother's hand-me-downs, including his shirts. My underwear and socks had holes in them. On the nights I wanted to look nice and go out, my sister would iron the cuffs. Only the cuffs! It was so bad I would wear a sweater even when it was hot – I wasn't taking that sweater off and exposing the wrinkled hand-me-down underneath.

There was this guy on the *TODAY Show* named Dave Garroway, who showed on *national* TV that he had holes in the elbows of his shirts, so naturally, I just assumed he came from my neighborhood!

But hand-me-downs were what we had, so that's what we wore. We never asked for anything new or fancy, because we knew chances were we weren't going to get it, and we didn't want to embarrass our parents. It didn't matter anyway – because *you don't miss what you never had*. What mattered was we had love and togetherness.

Another time, we had no money for a Christmas tree, but Mom was not going to let a little detail like that spoil Christmas for *her* kids. We might have been down on our luck, but we were going to have a tree! I don't know where she got it, or how, but she came home with a tree... sort of. It was the smallest tree I'd ever seen. As soon as she came through the door with the tree *in one hand* – we all burst into, "Oh Christmas shrub, Oh Christmas shrub..." But it didn't matter, because in our minds, she'd brought home the Rockefeller Center Christmas tree. We decorated it and stuck it up in the window. We were so proud.

Another Christmas, my brother Roy and I received a pack of socks from John's Bargain Stores, the kind that came with three pairs – so we split them. One pair each, along with a spare! John's Bargain Stores was in Jamaica, Queens. It's what we would call a flea market today, and we'd go there with my mom to shop. All of the neighborhood moms shopped there, so it was always an afternoon of socializing while finding the best buys for the bucks! It was on those shopping trips that all the kids learned about the random phone call PRIZE. To be honest, I don't remember what the prize was, but I remember we all wanted it! Which is why we *always* answered the phone with a cheery "John's Bargain Stores – Open Friday, Saturday and Sunday Sale Days!" Granted, it was a little odd, but that's how everyone in our neighborhood answered the phone – you couldn't take the chance and NOT win the prize!

It was probably these same shopping expeditions that made me start to take notice of, not fashion per se, but what I called *snappy dressers*. I have such a vivid memory of the day I took the train into Manhattan and saw men wearing beautiful leather shoes. Not the fake plastic stuff we had in my neighborhood that cracked and split in the cold and discolored your socks in the heat. Socks so cheap you had to place rubber bands around the tops so they wouldn't slip down and bunch up in your plastic shoes! No, these men had real leather shoes, made from soft, supple animal hide – the real-deal footwear. The day I first saw *those* shoes, I promised myself right there and then that I was going to work hard so I could one day buy a pair. Now, not a day goes by that I don't cherish my 100% leather (imported from Italy) shoes.

It was about this time another important lesson started to seep in: If you don't have it (money), you don't buy it... or you figure out how to *make do*!

How many people today have credit card debt? Folks, this isn't that hard to understand. If you don't have it, you can't buy it!

The Christmas shrub and John's Bargain Stores aren't isolated examples; my mother knew how to *make do*. I can remember her hocking her wedding ring to get the money for something she felt one of us needed. My father would go nuts when she did this!

Here's a thought about pawnshops: it's no accident that pawnshops are in poor neighborhoods or Vegas or places where people need money fast. Personally, I never understood the concept – "I'll take your ring and give you, how about, half of what it's worth? *But* if you don't bring back the money AND the exorbitant interest by the exact day and time I say, I own the ring. Which means I can sell it for more than double what I paid you to begin with!" (Note to self... rich people have lending institutions; poor people have pawnshops!)

This is probably a good place to let you know that during this journey, I'm likely to run off on a tangent (if you haven't figured that out by now). Usually it'll be about something that is bothering me, or something I just discovered, remembered, or randomly popped into my brain. It's like I'm having a party inside my head and I'm not inviting anyone – but it's freeing for me! My daughter likes to hear my wanderings; then again, she will remind me to stay on task. Honestly, I kind of like the way my mind works, but I will make an effort to reel it in!

With that said – back to my mom.

When my mom was working at the Gaiety Deli, every so often she would come home with half of a pastrami sandwich. It was a well-known secret that she probably picked it off a plate – someone's leftover – but we didn't care. We thought we had died and gone to heaven. It was stuffed so thick we could make two, maybe three sandwiches out of it. The excitement we all shared over such an unexpected feast is the memory I have, not the origin of the sandwich. I wouldn't trade those memories for the world. I've carried that lesson with me, too: *be joyful and appreciate what you DO have, rather than whining about what you DON'T*. Again, thanks Mom.

I'm sure there were families in our neighborhood who sat down for dinner and passed around serving dishes of vegetables and platters of *meat* as they talked about different subjects, then excused themselves and waited for dessert.

I'm also sure my daughter doesn't really believe the stories I've told her about my family's free-for-all meals – pancakes, corn griddles and Campbell's tomato soup – my favorite and the cheapest! Or beans and franks with fried bologna... and if we were lucky, a glass of Nestlé's chocolate milk to go with it (but only two teaspoons please, we have to make it last for everyone).

Truth was, my mom wasn't the best cook. In fact, she was a terrible cook! Her baked macaroni and cheese used to slide off the plate. But it was all we had, *so we ate it*. My sister still remembers how I'd occasionally find some individual macaroni in the cuff of my jeans that had either slid off the plate or I'd dropped in there on purpose to achieve clean plate status!

Then of course, there was the liverwurst. My mom would buy a BLOCK of liverwurst that would yield a week's worth of lunches for *all of us*. I didn't (and still don't) know where liverwurst comes from. Is it beef? Or pig? Or rat? And what end of the animal is it anyway? All I know for sure is it must be the cheap end.

Once, during lunch at school, I sat down next to this guy named Artie who was also eating a liverwurst and jelly sandwich, which got us laughing. Besides having the same gourmet lunch in common, he had holes in his socks too. Aaaah, I knew I'd found a kindred spirit. It's no surprise we became friends. To this day, when Artie and I get together, we *still* laugh about those liverwurst and jelly sandwiches.

Do I sound like my father now or what? ("When I was your age, we had to walk ten miles to school naked!") Which reminds me of something else my sister brought up to me – the phone lock. I don't mean blocked access like we have today, but an actual physical LOCK that my father put on the rotary dial of our phone (note: ONE phone in the whole house). My dad thought the phone should only be used for "important" things, so as far he was concerned, why would any of his kids need to use the phone? So I guess without even knowing it, he taught me *where there's a will there's a way*!

OK, for those of you who've never seen a rotary phone, much less used one, here's a quick review. Rotary phones came in either a table model or wall model, and on the body of the phone there was a small round disk which rested above the numbers and letters. There were ten holes cut in the disk so you could see each number (1 through 9, plus 0) under the disk. You'd stick your finger into each corresponding number hole and then *dial* the number you wanted the appropriate amount of times. Oh, and you only walked with the phone as far as the cord, which tethered the phone to the wall, would allow. The "receiver" itself was a small barbell-looking piece which you lifted to your ear to listen at one end and talk into at the other. When you lifted the receiver, two small buttons on the phone popped up, which made your connection, and when you hung up, the receiver pushed the buttons down, disconnecting your call.

Since the lock my dad put on the phone didn't affect the receiver, it didn't take me long to figure out how to make a call without his permission. I'd just pick up the receiver and tap the buttons up and down quickly until an operator (an actual live human being!) would politely get on the line with a cheery, "Operator, how may I help you?" I would tell her (operators were always female) I had a cast on my arm and couldn't dial the phone, and then I would tell her the number I wanted to call and she would connect me. BINGO! Score another cloaked lesson from Dad – *when life gives you lemons... make lemonade*!

My parents were married for fifty-four years and our home was filled with love and togetherness. Although I have to be honest and tell you the love wasn't enough for me. I always felt I needed more of that. Don't get me wrong; this isn't a condemnation, just a realization. Between the two of them working full-time jobs and raising four kids, there simply wasn't enough time or energy to go around for all of us. I whole-heartedly appreciate the fact my parents worked hard to provide the best they could to raise their children, and all in all, we kids *were* happy growing up.

A SEED IS SOWN

The only times I ever really got the sense that my parents were happy was when I'd see them laughing together watching TV. I particularly remember them cuddling on the couch, my dad holding my mom's feet, at 8:30 pm on Tuesday nights, watching *The Red Skelton Show* with Red playing singing cabdriver Clem Kadiddlehopper or cross-eyed seagulls Gertrude and Heathcliff, always ending each show with, "And may God bless." Those were special times.

Watching my parents laugh was partially why, at a young age, I decided what I wanted to do with my life. I wanted to make people laugh. For me, laughter meant happiness – and I wanted to make everyone happy!

Here's something else about TV shows back then: they were our (latchkey kids) benign babysitters. They were there to entertain and teach us – *My Little Margie, The Millionaire, Queen for a Day*. These were uplifting programs that set an example for all of us to reach higher, attain more, respect each other, be positive, dream, count our blessings, question everything, be kind and help the lesser person.

There weren't any shows where one person belittled and humiliated another person. People weren't rewarded for being rude or cruel or vulgar. Even if there had been, in our minds, *that* person would be the loser.

What *the hell* happened?!

It seems today, more and more people are not playing by the old rules and are just trying to disguise the truth by stretching and pulling it to suit their needs, which is further fueled and encouraged by what they see on TV.

Today, every show seems to anoint one person a Winner while everyone else is labeled a Loser! Shows like *The Apprentice, Survivor, Dancing With The Stars* and of course... *The Biggest Loser.*

Oh, don't even get me started on food shows! There are more slice-and-dice and braise- and-broil, worst cooks, best cooks, each promising big bucks while providing big humiliation – competition food shows on TV – than you can smack with a stick of butter. There are even shows dedicated to *nothing* but cupcakes. And everyone's sooo surprised our country has an obesity problem!

With the exception of a handful of shows today, everything put out as "entertainment" is just so far off the mark – it makes me cringe. Because actually, the only *truth* of reality shows is this: when you stoop so low as to sacrifice your soul by lying and doing whatever it takes to be the winner, *on a television show...* then you, my friend, are the biggest loser of all!

Oh right, you're a stripper working yourself through college or you're a single mom with a past dependency problem, or you're just a bored rich broad with too much time on your hands. Well, I knew women in my old neighborhood who had four kids and were working 12-hour shifts at a menial job while dealing with a drunkard of a husband who had gambled away the rent money and ran around with other women. But *those women* would never think of publicly demeaning another woman caught in the same circumstance, or sign on to prance around in their underwear, flirt with infidelity, or generally perform like a crazed bitch, all in exchange for five minutes of fleeting infamousness.

NO. *Those women* had integrity and pride and a moral compass to map out an actual plan to provide a good home *and* set an example for their kids they could be proud of!

Sorry, where was I?

Oh, yes... When I was about 12 or 13, we moved out to Long Island (my parents wanted to upgrade). Actually, it was more of a lateral move than an upward surge, but we did gain a driveway, a lawn and a tree. But still, my mom would send me to school with my lunch wrapped in a Silvercup bread bag that would break apart when I pulled out my peanut butter and jelly sandwich. The sandwich would fall to my knees and the other kids would all laugh. The rich kids had brown paper bags that were the perfect size for a sandwich, and their sandwiches were wrapped in plastic! (two ply... WOW... that was living!).

I also remember the jeans I wore to school. Back then, jeans weren't a fashion statement. They didn't have anyone's name scrolled across the ass – except maybe Levi. *Jeans were jeans.* They were plain blue denim, and mine had double-stitched knees and folded-up cuffs so I could wear them through *years* of growth spurts. Oh, the insults that came with those pants. "Hey, Farmer Schmuck! What are those cuffs for? To collect loose change?"

Now that I've shared a few examples of growing up – not just as another poor kid, but a kid bestowed with my father's New England principles and my mother's "just folks" attitude – let's take a look at how I modified (a little) what I learned, and how I applied it to surviving in New York City. New York City, where someone would rather shoot you over a parking spot than help you out; where a lawn is a patch of grass in front of your building used by every dog in the neighborhood (Ahh... that urine aroma on hot summer nights, I miss it so!); where a city cat wearing a leather jacket can stop a speeding subway train with its paw; and where being poor meant learning to read people quick – because there might not be another chance!

Principles were great, but they were out the window! In my mind, it was time to sink or swim. Survival was at-hand! But how do I turn the other cheek when there might not be another cheek? How do I bowl someone over with kindness when there might not be another day to bowl over anything but my gravestone? I had to make a choice: *Master* the game or lose it. I already knew the Right Way, but now I had to learn the Street Way.

See, I wish someone had sat me down a long time ago and shared with me all of these life lessons. It would have saved me a lot of time, heartache, money and searching... and while some people will never get it, I thank God I did.

Luckily, this was the time (and the place) it became apparent to me that I was the funny guy amongst my friends, and girls seemed to like a funny guy, so I figured those were good things. The added bonus was that I discovered I could disarm and charm just about anyone, including adults, by making them laugh.

Even after we moved to Long Island, my mom continued to be cuisine challenged. Which is why it didn't take too long for me to discover the concept of "eating over" at a friend's house – a discovery that probably had as much to do with my career choice as anything else.

To this day, I can tell you what time my friends' parents sat down for dinner and which ones had a place set for me at the table, just in case I happened to make an appearance that night. I'm not embarrassed to tell you I "ate over" at my friends' houses a lot. So what if I had to perform? Making their parents laugh to guarantee being asked back to partake in another honest-to-goodness meal was well worth it. I wasn't ashamed then, nor am I ashamed now. As a matter of fact, I found that I enjoyed being the "dinner show." I had a captive audience – the table/impromptu stage was mine! As long as I kept my stories fresh and funny, the food remained tasty. *Witness the true birth of a performer!*

By the time I graduated high school, I had decided I was going to dedicate my life to making people laugh. Before trying to figure out *how* to make that happen, my first priority was to get an education. I saw too many people from the old neighborhood lacking in so many ways, not just economically. They were simply stuck in a *job* with no avenue to ever advance because they couldn't afford a higher education for themselves, or couldn't provide any higher education for their families (besides, all those men with the nice-looking leather shoes looked educated to me!). I also figured that if the comedy thing didn't work out, I could always fall back on my education.

There was something else, too. For the first time in my life, I saw my dad as someone other than just my dad. I saw an older adult man. I could see how much life had frayed his edges, slowed his pace, and affected his health. That's when it really hit me... my dad *was one of those people*. He'd spent his entire life stuck in a *job*. A job that he was, by no means, ashamed of; he worked extremely long and hard to support his family, and he did so with grace, honesty and integrity, but it wasn't a job he loved.

It wasn't too long after this realization that my dad sat me down and proceeded to talk about my future. I listened as he talked about how things had changed since he was a young man; how there were so many more opportunities for kids these days and how I shouldn't rush in to anything right away.

24

After a couple of minutes, I asked him, "What do you think I should do with my life?"

His reply was almost immediate. "Do something you love, no matter what it is. If you love doing it, it won't seem like a job."

And there it was. All the proof I needed to reaffirm my conviction to carve out a life in comedy. Although he didn't say it exactly, I know he wanted all his children to find something *more* than what he had, to not just settle for a job. He wanted us to find our passion – a need and a desire – then go after it.

I took this last bit of wisdom and gently packed it on top of the stack of all the lessons I'd learned, as that poor kid from the streets of New York City, and headed out on my own journey through life.

Chapter 2
42°93' N, 78°73' W AND OTHER DESTINATIONS

My neighbor Mikey from the old neighborhood used to say, "Look both ways down a one-way street!" When people hear me say this now, they always ask, "What does that mean?"

Here's the best way to explain it. I left my family in Long Island and shuffled off to... the University of Buffalo (which has a *lot* to do with why I now live in sunny California). Now, I was no stranger to winter and snow, but I didn't have the wardrobe for "south of the bear!" So, like every other incoming student, I purchased THE parka – a coat guaranteed to keep you warm up to 40° below zero. It was an Eskimo-looking thing with fur sewn all around the hood. It looked like you were giving a fox a piggyback ride. When you pulled the hood over your head and zipped the parka up to your nose (which you had to do a lot of times because of the blinding snow) there was no way you could see on either side of you. It was like you were walking around as a down-filled Eskimo cannoli! We lost many students crossing the street with that coat on, "Hey, where's Freddie? What? Truck on Main Street? Can I have his room?"

You can't go through life wearing a parka, seeing only what's directly in front of you. You have to look both ways down a one-way street because if you don't, just like Freddie – BAM! People, or circumstances and situations, will blindside you. You'll be going along expecting things to go the way you planned and someone or something will bean you with a curveball – in short, you're fucked! Believe me, when you get bean-balled, the *dumb shit* doors fly open and self-blame comes chattering through with "What did I do wrong?" Right behind is guilt. "I should've seen this coming!" Or worse, the questions that have no answers. "Why does this always happen to me?" "Is there a cloud hanging over my head?" "Am I doomed?" To be honest, my own *dumb shit* doors rival a Chinese kitchen on Christmas day! But do I give up? *No!* Because I've learned that looking both ways always provides options to consider.

When you allow yourself to look in more than one direction, you *always* have a choice. I remember one old girlfriend who was always ahead of herself. She'd always set herself up... and me! Going out for dinner and a movie was never just a dinner and a movie. She saw our night as a magical fantasy – how great everything would be, how the food would taste, what we would talk about in the car ride over and the friends we would meet up with later that night. Up to that point in her life, no one ever told her to "Look both ways down a one-way street" – which is exactly what I wound up doing. I told her we might get stuck in traffic, the food could be served cold and the friends she was glowingly thinking of were actually the jealous types. She told me I was ruining everything and it was always my fault when our dates didn't turn out to be the *Love Channel* movie of the week!

But how could you go through life constantly setting yourself up for disappointment and resentment like that? Sure, it's nice to have a daddy who shields you and protects you as much as possible, but come on! The world is not a perfect place. Every time I looked up on the tote board to find her name, the word ISSUES kept popping up. Needless to say, we didn't last too long.

Not long ago, I ran into her. I hadn't seen her for years. Oh, was I shocked! If I hadn't recognized her voice, I wouldn't have had any idea who she was. Two minutes into the conversation, I understood the toll life had taken on her. She still only sees what she wants to see, which has made her an angry, bitter "old lady!" Thank God she still has daddy supporting her.

Most of what we see every day is merely a snapshot, a glimpse of any given personal encounter or situation. We only see what we want to see, without bothering to look deeper. But when the situation merits, wouldn't you rather *look* in order to discover the whole truth and deal with it – good or bad – than be satisfied with only what you see? Isn't it amazing how some of your friends always seem to be able to instantly *look* right into the core of something and *know* all they need in order to deal with the whole situation?

Maybe we're just afraid to take that extra step, to look deeper, because if we did we might actually discover something bad. And who wants to uncover the bad side of something or someone when everything is supposed to be like Disneyland?

How many times have you listened to someone tell an unflattering story about someone you know only to find yourself thinking, *I'm not surprised?* That's because, initially, you knew there was *something* about that person that bothered you. But for whatever reason, you ignored that something. You didn't bother to *look* deeper, and over the years that person morphed into a trusted friend. So what was it that bothered you? Probably, if you *had* taken the time to *look*, you would've discovered they were psycho! I'm not talking about the most obvious psychos – the guy who has twelve metal rings running across his eyebrows and when you meet him, you can't help but say, "You should put up a shower curtain there." I'm talking about the psychos who appear normal on the outside. Take Jeffery Dahmer. He looked like Jimmy Olsen after he clocked out, but then went home and ate people!

WHAT LIES BEHIND US AND WHAT LIES BEFORE US ARE TINY MATTERS COMPARED TO WHAT LIES WITHIN US.
—Ralph Waldo Emerson

After graduating from college, I still knew in my heart that what I really wanted was a life in comedy, but, I also knew a dream wasn't going to pay the bills! So while visiting my parents one day, I again asked my dad, "What should I do with my life?" Again, his answer was swift and short.

"You should go into sales. You're good with people. They like you. You should sell bridges."

So it's probably *not* a coincidence that one of my first "adult" jobs was working as a salesman for an American company selling Japanese steel back to American companies. Mind you, this was when American companies still weren't buying anything directly from Japan because of our past history. Funny, now, we buy everything from Japan – because it's cheaper. *Money is a powerful anesthetic.*

Following that, I kicked around trying this job and that. I even taught high-school history for a while and sold jewelry business-to-business until I made the jump back to New York City and became a "Garmento."

Yes, I was a Garmento (the term for someone whose life's work is the garment business). I became a Garmento because, in part, it left my nights free, which allowed me to venture into, and eventually begin, performing at comedy clubs around the city.

Had I not chosen to explore this new path toward comedy – had I remained a Garmento – I would've had to change my name to Murray, moved to Florida, been diagnosed with colon cancer (recovering nicely!), all so I could spend the rest of my days refereeing shuffleboard games on the beach for nickels and smoking three packs of Marlboros a day.

Besides, being a Garmento paid the bills, and I was good at it. Man, was I good at it! I *quickly* learned that people *buy the person and not the product.* Granted, the product has to be decent, but really, what's a shirt or a blouse? Just some material and a few buttons. Fact is, a customer can buy those anywhere. So what makes the difference in their purchasing decision? *You* make the difference. They're buying you!

In truth, my day job turned out to be excellent training for "selling" an audience on my comedy and me. But I wasn't

29

ready to give up a steady, well-paying job selling garments just yet. So, for the first year and a half that I did comedy, I kept my Manhattan Garmento job. Knowing I had a steady income, I was able to spend every night trying everything I could to get on that stage, but clubs wouldn't even let me catch swine flu in the beginning! Most of the time I'd just take dates to *Catch A Rising Star* and sit and watch the other comics on stage. I'd get to see David Brenner, Gabe Kaplan or Freddie Prinze, Jr. hanging out at the bar (which at the time was a thrill for me) and every now and then this new guy Robin Williams would stop in and try out some material, along with a host of other comics we've all come to recognize as household names, including Jerry Seinfeld, Drew Carey, Chris Rock and Rosie O'Donnell.

When I watched these guys perform, my energy level would literally go through the roof! I knew in my heart *this* is what I needed to do with my life and *this was the club* I needed to be doing it at. It's like when you're getting married, you don't stop and you ask yourself, "How do I know this is the right person for me?" You just know – that's how you know! *By the way, if you DO have to stop and ask yourself if the person you're about to marry is the right person – odds are they ARE NOT!*

After gaining enough stage time at clubs, I felt the time had come for me to make a decision. I could keep working as a Garmento and occasionally do comedy, or I could drop the net and go after my dream. The decision was easy; the reality – not so much. But I left the security of my Garmento life behind to devote myself to becoming a full-time comedian.

As I said before, *the* place to perform and be seen was *Catch A Rising Star,* a comedy club on 76th Street and 1st Avenue in New York City. The one thing that I hadn't anticipated was the jealousy, backstabbing and fighting that goes on just to get stage time. This is something they refer to in the business as "paying one's dues." These people would literally kill their own mother to get a paid working spot on the weekend. They would shake your hand with their right while sharpening a knife with their left. It was so bad that I wanted to cleanse myself with a chicken! Old naïve Bobby was under the impression that we were all one big, talented family wanting to make the world laugh and maybe, just maybe, help people forget about their lives for a while by coming into our wacky universe. WOW, was I wrong! It was a daily struggle just to make friends, let alone trust anyone. Damn it! I thought this business of comedy would be different. But hey, I had rolled up my sleeves and learned the Garmento business (leaving quite accomplished, too) so... let the games begin!

I remember one night, after a show, I was talking to this guy – he wasn't a comic, but unfortunately I don't remember

Bobby on stage at a California corporate gig. "White men can dance!"

his name, which is funny, considering the profound effect he's had on my life – so let's just call him Stan. Anyway, I must've had a bad night because Stan and I were talking when I suddenly went off on a rant, complaining about how I wasn't getting any good spots at *Catch*. I went on and on about how I'd be up there at one o'clock in the morning (the shit spot you get as a newbie!) performing to a "crowd" of maybe seven drunks, and one of them would always put his head down and start snoring right in front of me! And if that weren't bad enough, the Chinese cleaning guy would start vacuuming the place right in the middle of my set! As quickly as I'd first started, I stopped and asked Stan, "How is any of this helping me to learn my craft?" To which, he replied, "Why not just go to another club?"

What? Clearly Stan didn't understand! He wasn't in this field! This was *the* club to be at! Why was I even asking him for advice?! But you know what? Stan was right and I was wrong. Another club was exactly what I needed. I was obviously hitting a wall at *Catch* and could get more stage time somewhere else. So I decided to go to this beautiful new club called *Caroline's* that had just opened on 28th Street & 8th Avenue. And when I walked into *Caroline's* that first time, *I completely understood* – I hadn't been looking both ways down a one-way street!

YOUR WAY, MY WAY AND THE RIGHT WAY

For me, learning to *look* at everything I see has not come without pain, because once you DO, you have to determine a way to handle what you find out! Being brought up under my father's New England puritanical principles, I was always told, "Do unto others as you would have others do unto you." I was taught to respect your elders, never lie and above all – always take responsibility for your actions (which more times than not *really* meant... there's Your Way and then there's MY Way!

There were some people, comics and others, who, early

in my career, were not kind; who stabbed me in the back, both figuratively and emotionally. Well, through some trial and error, I developed *another* way to make others aware of their responsibility for their own actions... the *Right Way*.

Which is why, on those occasions when I run into someone from those early days, I will look in their eyes only to get back a stare which reads, "That's all I knew back then and that's the way it was!" Or with some others, their eyes practically shout, "I still don't get it and probably never will!" I don't lecture them, or ask why they behaved the way they did; I *try* to handle matters the *Right Way*! I offer them a smile and a pleasant "Hello." I set an example the *Right Way*, and keep moving!

While in principle this *seems* simple enough to follow, you know as well as I do... this ain't always easy! Have you been out in the world lately? ACCKKK! There's no shortage of whack-jobs wearing goggles and living in domes thinking one day they're going to meet their future spouse on a TV show ("*The Bachelor* is going to pick me!"). Well, all I can say is – forget about it and good luck! But wait, before you're done entertaining your crazy person, come see me because I have a bridge I need to sell you. Sorry, but I did say I'm *trying* to handle things the Right Way, didn't I? In the end, the bottom-line is: shit floats for a while, then it sinks, but cream always rises to the top!

As my career grew, I can easily count the number of times when I thought I had a special gig or TV show in my hands. The deal was so close I could taste it. And boy, did I want it! Then BAM! Something changed and it was gone. Did I feel disappointed? You bet I did. Did I wallow in my misfortune, even briefly? You bet I *didn't*. Why? Because if I spent my valuable time trying to figure out all the reasons why I didn't get something, I might miss out on the next gig or the next TV show that *I'm supposed to get*. You can't control what is out of your control; you just have to move on! The fact that you came so close this time only proves you're going to get it the next time. Instead of being disappointed, you should be excited for the next opportunity to come around. Just keep putting the same message out there and let the universe do its thing.

I have a friend who is a writer. I've always envisioned him sitting in a room in his house, like Rob Petrie from *The Dick Van Dyke Show,* coming up with ideas and dialogue for TV shows. I remember running into him many years ago when he was down on his luck. He told me he couldn't find any work; that he'd sent his writing everywhere with no luck. He went on to say that money was getting real tight and that he might need to sell his house. I asked him if he could be doing anything else other than what he'd already tried. He asked me what I meant, so I told him, "Well, you've done everything you could in that field to find a job and nothing is coming, so maybe you should do something else. You know, look both ways down a one-way street."

I went on to tell him as long as you're putting something, anything, created from positive energy out there, something positive will come back. Maybe not come back from where you *thought* you were looking, but *something* will come!

Eventually, my writer friend took a job as an editor for a script company (just to stir the pot). There was no money in it, but guess what happened? Not only did he get great ideas from reading those scripts, but he also helped select a few projects to write and produce. And one of those projects hit it big, turning him into the executive producer of one of the longest-running sitcoms in the history of television! Has he ever called me up to offer me a thing? Absolutely not! But remember, I helped him the Right Way, by pointing out the importance of looking both ways down a one-way street. And because I did it the Right Way, I know it will come back to me. Will it come from him? I doubt it. But the point is, it will come back to me and when it does, it will be the right message presented to me in the Right Way – which never would have been seen, except when looking both ways down a one-way street!

Bobby and Kevin Nealon at The Comedy & Magic Club, Hermosa Beach, California. "Got weed?"

Chapter 3
GOOD THINGS HAPPEN WHEN YOU GET YOUR PRIORITIES STRAIGHT

RELIGIONS ARE A REFLECTION OF WHO MAN THINKS GOD IS, WHICH IS USUALLY WRONG. THE BEST WAY TO KNOW WHO GOD REALLY IS, IS TO OBSERVE NATURE, KNOW WHO YOU ARE, BE WHO GOD CREATED YOU TO BE AND WHO GOD IS WILL SHOW UP.
—Candi Taylor-Jeter

There was a time in my life if you said you wanted to talk to me about God, I'd answer, "Sorry, not in my top 100 subjects." And church? Church was something my mother made us attend when we were younger. I never understood Latin and always had to look down the pew to the other people just to figure out when it was time to sit/stand/kneel. It always felt like gym class. "OK, stand. Now sit. OK, down on your knees. Now stand again. But this time, do some push-ups and squat thrusts while saying two Hail Marys and four Our Fathers, and one genuflection before you're done." The guilt was rampant and all planned by the priests, then endorsed and sanctioned by our parents!

Just a sidebar: I went to Easter Sunday this year, and do you know the church bulletin has grown to become a marketer's dream? You can now advertise for a casket on the back of the bulletin – *now that's one-stop shopping!* Imagine the advertising campaign, "When you have too much guilt crowding your life and your chest pains are becoming stronger, odds are you're going to die. But don't worry, Heathen & Benny's can help you choose a casket your family will be proud of." The priest's vestments also now have promotional logos on them. I was taking communion and Ronald McDonald's face was on the sleeve of the robe. I thought I was receiving a McHost. I recently saw one for Gallo Wine. Seriously, it's *scary*. Talk about hypocrisy!

36

Anyway, growing up, it always seemed to me that the whole point of church was to instill *the fear of God into us!* But even back then a donation could always wipe away that fear. See, there's always a price! And it worked pretty well, too. My entire childhood I was scared to death! But in my heart, I think I always knew the way it should be: that the relationship between church and God, the way it was taught to me, *wasn't* the way. Because to me, the "taught way" had no net! I'm not just talking about Catholicism; I'm also talking about all these people who get involved in Buddhism, Judaism, Scientology, Mormonism, born-again Christians – I guess, basically *any* organized religion. Because when you see these people talking about their devoted practice, there's always something missing – *like the brain cell for logic!*

I always knew the way the Catholic Church was "operating" would have to be addressed someday. And boy has their day ever come around! Talk about catching the fox in the henhouse! All I can say is, "Thank you, God. I *knew* you wouldn't let this go on forever." But who am I to question your time frame? You're driving the bus; I'm just here for the ride.

Through my education and later, as I traveled around, I came to understand that there had to be a better way than what I learned growing up. Primarily because that whole, "There's only One Way and *our* way is THE One Way" pronouncement really gets to me. And what kills me the most about it is *that's what they all say!* The Catholics, the "born agains" (what, they didn't get that birth thing right the first time?), the people in orange (I like orange, but I'm no "rainbow man"), Scientology (no, I'm not jumping on Oprah's couch!) and let's not leave out those people who look like they've never paid a mortgage. All these churches tell you, "WE are THE way!" Well, I have to tell you, "Nope. None of them is for me." The way for each of us starts in our hearts, because doesn't it all come from the inside out and not the outside in? Hey, just because I don't believe in churches doesn't mean I've never listened to God!

I know deep in my soul how things really are, and it's not the way people make them out to be. There's too much evidence on my side. Like the times I knew something I

37

couldn't possibly have known, yet without a doubt, I *knew* it to be true. Sometimes, I can see things with absolute clarity, but I have no clue as to why. It's like 99% of what we don't see is reality and the 1% we do see is where we live. Boy, do we make it hard on ourselves! Makes you wonder – when you hear we only use a small percentage of our brain that if we could really *see everything* around us and process it, if we might actually explode. I can see it now: people passing each other on the street, their heads going off like M-80's, and all you'd hear are strangers saying, "I know, it's sad. But he just saw too much! He just couldn't handle it!"

Not too long after I started working as a full-time comedian, a friend of mine asked me to go with her to meet a person she described as a spiritual man – a person who could see beyond this life into the future; a seer. Of course, I allowed my New England logic and New York skepticism to take over and advised her not to fall prey to any of this "New Age" metaphysical mumbo jumbo. I could hear my father telling me, "They only want your money!"

Hey, we're all searching, but in order to really find your true path you have to lift your foot off the base every once in a while and see what's out there. So, I told myself, "Bobby, don't be a dinosaur; *be open*. It's good to look at who you really are so you can see if what you're experiencing is the real deal." I also think God (at least my God - a loving and kind God) would expect me to test him every now and then so that I know he's real – even without all the repetitive words, group affiliation, money and bullshit!

There's an old saying, "When the student is ready, the teacher appears." To this day, I thank God for leading me down the path that guided me to this man. See, things do happen for a reason! There *is* a plan. Even as I'm writing these words, I can't believe I'm talking about my own past – but it's true.

The *second* I met this man I knew we were supposed to meet. Never in my life had I been so comfortable with someone that quickly. Wait a minute, just so we're clear – I'm no *Brokeback Mountain* or Moonie, or at the very least, even a follower. But when this man looked into my eyes, I knew he could see my soul. I can't explain it, but that's what happened. He was an extraordinary person, a special man. I knew that people like him existed, but I'd never met anyone like him. I was taken aback. I wanted to savor the moment. This was special and I knew it. This was magic – the Easter Bunny, Santa Claus and the Tooth Fairy all rolled into one! And he looked like an everyday person. Thank God, because if he looked any other way, I would have never given him a second glance.

I put myself "on" for this man, just so he would like me. This is something I'd never done before (or since) for anyone. Well, maybe a little, when I need to get an upgrade at the airport or deal with a customer service representative face-to-face or hide the fact that I know nothing about home repairs or cars! But I never took it to the level that I did just to make sure this man would like me. Without hesitation, I knew he understood what I was thinking and feeling, which was: *I need more in my life.* I knew I was on the right path, because suddenly someone, God or whomever, gave me an invisible slap to the back of the head, as if to say, "What are you waiting for? This is the right time. This is the right man. THIS is the shot in the ass you've been searching for!" So, I asked this man, "What's the answer?"

With smiling eyes, he gently said, "God." To which, I replied, "Thank you!" He knew I wanted to scream and shout, "Finally! Someone who can cut right through all the bullshit and give me the information I need to hear the way I need to hear it!" I wanted to call *all* my friends and share the experience with them because I figured they'd be as excited as I was; that they were at the same place to welcome what he'd shared with me.

Well, it turns out – *no*, we're not all at the same place at the same time. But I did share with a lot of them... and you know what? They all thought I was going nuts!

On that first night we met, this man also asked me if I was a clown. Thinking he'd misunderstood what I'd told him, I felt I needed to clarify myself, so I repeated my intention was to perform stand-up comedy on a stage and not under a tent in the circus. To which he replied, "That's what you should be doing with your life." *Ahh...* confirmation! He also told me I would be married twice, have two children and I would have to keep a careful eye on my firstborn. I told him I was about to get married for the first time, to which, he just rolled his eyes and said, "This is just what I see." Fast-forward twenty-five years to the present – I'm now married to my second wife, I have two children and we have had challenges with our firstborn daughter.

I've seen so many people – rich, poor, middle-class, celebrity, politicians, *you name it* – come see this man for a reading. His gift was to tell the truth about what he saw or what was told to him; some walked out happy, others walked out sad and crying, while others just walked out confused. For everyone who went to see him, they were given the choice to use the information he told them and apply it to their own life as they saw fit. He was the most gifted messenger on this planet we call Earth. I loved him very much and even though he's passed on, I think of him every day. Only now when I speak to him, I tell him how much I miss him and that I know he's not too far away.

Ever since the day I met this man, I work at making sure I keep God as my first priority, because when you try and use a different line-up, placing family or career before God – you will find yourself having to get back on where you got off!

I'd like to point out that I don't consider myself a "My Way or the Highway" kind of guy. However, when an opportunity presents itself, I definitely take the time to share my own truths with someone – *God First, Family Second, Career Third*. Usually, when I tell this to someone, they *get* it. I can see the light bulb going on! But if they don't get it, I take comfort in knowing that they eventually will, just when they need it the most... and not a minute before.

I was backstage at a venue one time, talking with the opening comic, and he was telling me how much he appreciated being on the same bill, and I reciprocated. During our conversation, he asked, "How do you handle your career and your family? Especially in this business, isn't your family a burden?"

"Why are they a burden?"

He goes on to tell me how wonderful his girlfriend is; how she wants to spend time with him; how she feels he's the right guy to start a family with, but he's not sure, because money will be tight and he'll be on the road, and all their conversations are just making him feel pressured. As he's telling me all this, I'm thinking, *Oh he's not ready. He's not willing to put family before career.*

I've often been tempted during other conversations to share this truth with even more people (more than I already do), but most of the time, I don't, because I know the other person will most likely react the same way I did at one time, "OK, pal... whatever you say! Where did ya pull that one from? Outta your ass?"

Here's the kicker: many of the people I've shared these truths with wind up coming to me later on, letting me know that what I said to them was *exactly* what they needed to hear at that moment in their life. At first, this surprised me and made me a bit uneasy, but it has since given me a great deal of satisfaction knowing that I acted upon what I heard in my head and then put my own truth out there. It makes my heart feel good!

SUCCESS IS NOT THE KEY TO HAPPINESS. HAPPINESS IS THE KEY TO SUCCESS. IF YOU LOVE WHAT YOU ARE DOING, YOU WILL BE SUCCESSFUL.
    —Herman Cain (Yup – the same Herman Cain)

I love what I do for a living! I love traveling around the country and making people laugh! I'm circus people. Good old-fashioned carnie folk. I pull into a town, put on a show and make 'em laugh, pull up stakes and move on to the next town. The history books would call someone like me a gypsy or a court jester. On second thought, they'd probably just call me a moron! I don't care; I love being a stand-up comedian. It's *my* path, and I've been on it for thirty incredible years. It's just like any business, but in this one, the people are colorful, intelligent, insightful and truthful – although I have to admit, the *constant* traveling sucks!

But I do love the actual performing. It's a rush – a NEED to get up on stage, to open the pathway to my stories, to share my observations of what is funny and what is folly and all that's in between. To put it all (everything) out there and let everyone know that not only is it okay to laugh at the human condition, but it's healing and healthy to do so. To share *my* view of life, *my* perspective of people and the everyday world, *and* get paid for it... what a trip!

I have to admit, though, sometimes, I double guess my vocation choice.

The yang to the yin of my life rears its ugly head. When I least expect it or want it, I wind up having self-criticizing, self-doubting conversations with myself filled with unanswerable questions like, *What the hell am I doing with my life? Why don't I get a real job? Shouldn't I be at an office somewhere in a meeting right now?* But you know what I say to those questions?

Fuck it! I love the feeling I get from performing my craft.

Even after all these years, there are still times when my ego tries to get the upper hand and tempt me to think about placing my career before God and my family. *How stupid is that?* So even though I *know* God is driving the bus, every once in a while, I find myself jumping out of my seat and running to the front to talk to the driver. "Hey, God. There's this guy and he can do a lot for my career. He's a big shot in the business – *by the way, I think we should make a left turn up here* – he's rich and powerful and I can actually get an appointment to see him." But then I have to stop myself by saying, "Oh, wait. You're God! You always know what's best for me. Sorry, it's that party in my head thing again where I think I can do it my way without my family, without anyone – even without you!"

I guess these moments of doubt are just my cross to

bear, and we all have one. But maybe that's why we *all* have some doubts in the first place: to help us find our way through all of this living nonsense in order to strengthen our convictions and remind us of our priorities!

Just to be clear, your career is what you do, it's not who you are. Never place your career ahead of God or your family. But if you forget, and in the short run you leap ahead and put career first, make sure you don't get caught up in that feeling that leads you to believe you have this "life thing" all figured out. Because in no time, you'll see how WRONG you are!

Eventually, you have to get back on where you got off. *Trust me.* I know what I'm talking about with this one!

NEVER MISTAKE KNOWLEDGE FOR WISDOM. ONE HELPS YOU MAKE A LIVING, THE OTHER HELPS YOU MAKE A LIFE.
—Sandra Carey

I've seen my career jump way out there, only to turn around and see my family suffering because of a temporary change in the batting order.

Like the time I received a phone call for a part in a new television show pilot. I was *ecstatic*, feeling great. Once again, the universe was showing me that great opportunities always come back around! After I hung up the phone, I remember thinking – *OK, this is what I've been waiting for!* Then a few days later, when I spoke to the producer, he tells me the shoot is on Tuesday night. I respond, "Hold on. I'm leaving for a Caribbean vacation with my wife and kids on Tuesday morning. Can we shoot it on Monday night instead?" He replies, "No, the shoot is on Tuesday night. Sorry." As excited as I was at first, Tuesday was no good for me, so I had to tell him I couldn't make it. My wife and kids come first. While this was a very difficult thing to say, I felt the strength and conviction of my decision in my soul. In the past – *when I had no sense* – I would've cancelled the vacation, lost money and disappointed my wife and kids, all so I could pursue my own dream *separate* from them. Now I know my dream would have meant nothing if I'd handled it that way. Which is to say, the wrong way! I've learned over the years that when you do things the Right Way, it always works out for the best.

By the way, that show never made it to air, but the vacation was fantastic!

ACHIEVEMENT RESULTS FROM WORK REALIZING AMBITION. —
Adam Ant (that's right – Adam Ant)

I started to see some success come my way, taking me further and further away from my dysfunctional family and my poor childhood. I found myself traveling on tours with Cher, Julio Iglesias, Dolly Parton and Tony Bennett. I also hosted my own TV show on VH1 called *Stand-Up Spotlight*. Around the same time, I became the national spokesperson for Certs breath mints, riding in limousines (playing with the windows like it's nobody's business!), staying in hotels with heated towel racks and having breakfast at restaurants that charge $23 – TWENTY-THREE DOLLARS! – for a glass of orange juice. I became exposed to so many people and situations that were never a part of my life growing up that it's ridiculous. A part? They weren't even bit players!

It was also around this time that I purchased my first pair of new leather shoes, the same beautiful leather shoes I saw on the train to Manhattan all those years ago as a kid. Dreams do come true!

NOTHING MAKES IT EASIER TO RESIST TEMPTATION THAN A PROPER BRINGING-UP, A SOUND SET OF VALUES – AND WITNESSES.
—Franklin P. Jones

Now, I know some of you may be wondering about the validity of the tabloid tales perpetuated about professional entertainers – *I'm talking about women!* I've had too many guys – and women – over the years come up to me after a show and ask, "Bobby, what about all the ladies out there? Huh? Huh?" The rag mags are filled with tales of celebrity infidelity and affairs of opportunity. Don't get me wrong, I see the women out there. Beautiful women, with bodies like blossoms (especially since women are a huge part of my audience). And while I appreciate their support, *that's as far as it goes*. I'm polite, I engage in pleasantries and move on. I prefer to tend my own secret garden and leave the gathering of wildflowers to the young and single.

Dolly Parton and Bobby, Caesar's Palace. "Well, Helloooo, Dolly!"

EVERYONE WHO ACHIEVES SUCCESS IN A GREAT VENTURE SOLVES EACH PROBLEM AS THEY CAME TO IT. THEY HELPED THEMSELVES. AND THEY WERE HELPED THROUGH POWERS KNOWN AND UNKNOWN TO THEM AT THE TIME THEY SET OUT ON THEIR VOYAGE. THEY KEEP GOING REGARDLESS OF THE OBSTACLES THEY MET.

—W. Clement Stone

A full and successful life right now means being able to spend time with my family and the people who are important in my world. My career provides ample means, which allows me to provide for my wife and daughters, and also gives me time to sit and talk, particularly with my second-born daughter, who, because of her physical limitations, can't speak. When I see the joy and love she has on her face for her daddy, it reminds me that I have the most worthy and true accomplishments I can ever wish to claim.

So, while it has taken me a long time to reach this level in my career, I know in my heart, by continuing to adhere to my priorities – *God First, Family Second, Career Third*, my success will only continue.

Chapter 4
WHAT GOES AROUND COMES AROUND

My grandmother had a saying, "What goes around comes around." From the time I was a young boy, I remember hearing her say that all the time. She would also refer to something called karma. I would think, *How strange, someone can't tell the difference between a car and his ma?* (Oh, come on! That one was just sitting there!) Being a good kid, I'd listen to my grandmother, even though I didn't quite understand the part about always staying positive and doing good deeds so that the universe will reward you when you need it. But even back then, the whole idea sounded great to me!

If karma does exist – *and it does* – I'm guessing at the bottom of the karmic totem pole is the annoying son-of-a-bitch. You know, the kind of person who goes out of their way to talk to you only so they can have something bad to share with others later on when you're not around. I'm not talking about constructive criticism here – we've all given that out from time to time. I'm talking about someone who reeks of genuine mean-spirited negativity! Doesn't that person understand all the harmful stuff they spew out into the universe is only going to come back to them sooner or later? Obviously not, because once you open yourself up and see the bigger picture, you understand that this type of destructive behavior is exactly what keeps small-minded people stuck in the same place in life. It's like a dog chasing its own tail, going around and around, but never getting anywhere.

Witnessing your own "come around" and learning an important lesson you'll never repeat is life-changing.

Prime example: a guy from the old neighborhood asked me to hold onto something for him in my garage. Right away, my heart is saying, "No, I'm sorry. I've moved on." But my head is saying, "Bobby, he's from the old neighborhood. Help the guy out. Isn't that the right thing to do?" I tell Jill about my friend's request and also about the tug-of-war going on in my

48

"Bobby, you got any salsa sauce? I love you, Bobby!"

head. She responds (in that very high-pitched voice of reason only she has), "Bobby, will you stop with the 'old neighborhood' shit! There's nothing wrong with extending a hand, but you need to discriminate who it is you're extending it to."

I knew she was right. In the end I listened to my heart and didn't take his stuff, but I was still holding onto my past allegiance – a *false* allegiance, no less – but I've gotta tell you, it was STRONG!

A week later, I read in the paper this same guy was

caught with stolen goods. Right away, I'm thinking, "Oh my God! I could have been an accomplice!" Overnight, I'd have been Bobby "Baby Face" Nelson. In my head, I'm already talking like James Cagney, "Kids, whatever you do, don't follow the path I did! Just say no when that old pal you haven't talked to in a while asks you to help him out." I was convinced my house was going to be surrounded by the SWAT team and they were going to come crashing through my windows at any moment with guns blazing! OK, so I love a little touch of the drama, but I was definitely nervous!

As educational as this "come around" proved to be, there have been many times since where being the instrumental domino in someone else's "goes around" is even better.

Like the time I had this gig in Nashville, Tennessee, just as Nashville was coming into its own. The whole place was bustling – the music industry, hotels, upscale restaurants, you name it. The town was like a teenager thinking it was a lot more than it actually was, which meant some of the folks there could use a little kick in the ass to get them back in line!

Before I went to work at this club, some comic friends of mine told me, "This is a good place. The people there are pretty hip about life. You'll like it." But I gotta tell you, I was seriously questioning their endorsement as I was sitting alone in my hotel room at 7:48 pm waiting to hear from *anybody* at the club for a show that started at 8:00 pm. When the phone finally rang (and before I even had a chance to say "Hello"), this annoying voice with a thick Southern drawl on the other end says, "Where the hell are you?"

I reply, "Well, yes. Hi, to you too. This is Bobby Collins. My trip in was great. I can't tell you how excited I am that we'll be working together this weekend. By the way, there isn't anything I need on stage for my set."

CLICK!

After I take a cab over to the club, I walk in to meet the owner, who turned out to be the annoying voice on the other end of the phone. Before we're even formally introduced, I realize I already know this guy – I've met his type so many times during my career. He's one of those short, skinny,

50

power-hungry, Southern redneck types, *I've-been-doing-this-a-long-time assholes!* And it's guys like him who remind me sometimes doing stand-up comedy is actually nothing more than just a job.

In spite of the fact I have to deal with this less-than-perfect owner – let's just call him Opie – there are two things I immediately like about the club. First, there is a nice balcony in the room and second, there's a piano player on stage with me throughout my whole set. When I first started out in this business, there was always a piano player in the clubs. His job was to play to the audience before each show and also "play" each comic on and off the stage throughout the night. Every once in a while, he'd also play a little *emphasis* if he saw an opportunity to fit it into what you were saying (without distracting the audience or disrupting your material). Seeing a piano man again, I thought maybe this club might be fun after all.

As I'm waiting backstage in the "green room" for my turn to go on – which also happens to be Opie's office – I first hear and then watch as Opie launches into a tirade. He "goes off" on some poor young waitress who'd made a mistake on a drink tab. Now, I've heard club owners yell at employees before, but never in my life had I heard someone yell at another person the way this guy was screaming at this waitress! He was completely demolishing the poor girl! It didn't seem to matter to him that everyone could hear what he was saying, much less the fact that he was ripping her apart in front of the headliner, who was going to be working his club all weekend. As his rant goes on, I'm thinking, *OK, maybe she's a new waitress... or possibly he's having a bad day... or he was just served with divorce papers... or his father danced nude in front of his crib too much when he was a baby!* But still, this is not the way you treat another human being! While I wanted to get involved, that voice inside my head was saying, *Bobby, this is not your fight.*

A few minutes after the dust settles, I heard Opie do the same thing to another kid. A waiter this time, who earlier had told me he looked up to Opie. Sitting there, witnessing Opie's latest barrage of bile, I look at this kid and think, *Why in the world would you ever look up to such a piece of shit?*

After my first set is over, I'm once again back in the green room when the waitress from before walks in. We talk a little more and I learn she's been working at the club for over three years. I'm thinking, *Boy, the choices people make for themselves!* That's when she sheepishly adds, "Oh, yeah. I'm also not *allowed* to speak to the headliner. I'll get in troub..."

Too late. At that exact moment, Opie flies into the office and starts going off on this poor waitress again. Forget the reason this girl suddenly finds herself the victim of "Opie the Terrible." The point is she's someone's daughter or possibly someone's sister. Hell, she could be *my* sister. And you just don't treat my sister like that! There's also that whole thing about protecting someone who can't protect herself (or himself). That's why I believe this situation was unfolding right in front of me. It was up to me to handle it!

After Opie's latest verbal attack is over, this girl was crying and hovering in the corner and all I can think of is that Opie reminded me of one of those guys you see driving those huge 18-wheelers, the kind of guy you figure must be a big "breaker-breaker" type tough guy. You know, the rugged types that hunt down their own dinner rather than go to the supermarket or a restaurant like the rest of us. The type that uses a tree for a toothpick. WRONG! These guys are actually the little cancerous moles on your back. The ones that if they ever got into a fight, would fake left and then kick you right in the groin! I understand we're sharing the planet with a lot of different people, but the Opies of the world are all the more reason we have to start thinning out the herd!

I spent the rest of the weekend at this club "just doing my job." And outside of my initial phone call with Opie, and watching him dress down the staff in front of me, I didn't talk directly to him again until Saturday night. After my second sold-out show (which brought the total number of sold-out performances for the weekend to four), he came over to me and boasted, "The added third show is sold out!"

Now, in my contract (which Opie signed) it states the

option to perform a third show was up to the performer – ME! Since I've already decided I was never coming back to this club again, and I also figured there are just some people you're never going to be able to get along with, I told Opie, "Thanks, but I'm going to take a pass. Two shows are plenty for me." It's sad to say, but for some people, the Almighty Dollar is their God and the only way to make them stop and take notice is to spit on their deity! It's safe to say I definitely landed a big fat juicy loogie on Opie's golden calf!

Oh, the look on his face *was priceless*. And before I can even stop myself, I say, "What? It's not like I dug up the remains of your mother and had sex with her skull!" OK, granted, this might've been a tad harsh, but at this point in the weekend, all I wanted to do is really piss him off – and this seemed like a surefire way to do that!

Once Opie got his bottom jaw back in place, he responded, "This is all cash for you and you're telling me you're not going to do the show?"

"That's right," I answered. "I'm *not* doing the show."

As you can imagine, the rest of our conversation didn't go too well. To further demonstrate just what a "class act" he was, he made me wait around the hour it took him to return all the money to the people who'd paid for the third show. Finally, after everyone left, I went into his office to settle up (get my money) and I found him sitting behind his desk with his bartender standing over his right shoulder and his floor manager standing over his left shoulder.

"I'd like to have my money now," I told him.

"You chose not to do the third show," he responded. "So, I'm choosing *not* to pay you."

It's safe to say, I was totally blown away by this! This little shit of a man, who's perched up on his pleather toilet throne, with his flunkies standing guard, was telling *me* that I'm not getting paid!

Taking a breath, I leaned over his desk and calmly told him, "Oh, I'll get my money! Don't you worry!" This is where the New York street kid in me just wanted to take this little turd with both hands and kick his ass right there! Instead, I straightened up, walked out of his office and immediately called my agent at ICM.

"Bobby, don't worry about it," my agent reassured me. "I'll get your money."

"No," I responded. "I told that little shit I'd get my money... and I will get it!"

The next day, I took the first plane out of Nashville and in no time immersed myself back into my life in New York.

THE WAY IT WORKED

What happens a lot of times in this business is that you're asked by all types of non-profits to perform at their event at no charge (to give back) – schools, police departments, fire departments, community organizations. And being a parent of a special needs child, I'm particularly drawn to children's events. Not to get all sappy, but my belief is that if God gives you an angel with a clipped wing – wow – that's a big honor. So, anytime my schedule allows me to help out a children's organization by using the gift God gave me, I do so by performing free at their event, or at least participating in some way.

But to be completely honest, not every performance I do outside of a club is for a children's non-profit or the church choir. Through my non-club gigs, I've met all kinds of people – rich, poor, social climbers, false friends, kings, presidents and corporate CEOs – but I've also met my share of Klingons, drug lords, bookies and thugs! Generally, this last batch is full of good hard-working people who care about the same things you and I care about, but for whatever reason, decided to live life a different way. But they're not all "bad" people.

You can generally tell if someone is "bad" by the way they introduce themselves. I was once asked by a buddy of mine to stop by a private party that was being thrown for this lady. Her son had sent some work my way, so I wanted to duck in and wish her a happy birthday. I asked my friend Frank to join me and when we get there, we were ushered to a table in the middle of the room. As soon as we sat down, Frank leaned over to me and in his best stage whisper asked, "Bobby, do these people kill other people? They're all named after body parts – Tony "The Foot," Guido "The Arm, " and so on.

After the guest of honor stopped by our table, I wished her "Happy Birthday," and then we stuck around for a while so I can tell a few stories (that's what I do!). After the toast is

Mike Tyson and Bobby, MGM, Las Vegas. "I had two ears when I came in here..."

is finished and we're making our way to the door to leave, I heard Frank say, "It was nice to meet you, too, Mr. Foot." Back in the car, Frank looked at me and said, "What should I have said? I was just being polite! They all looked like characters out of *Goodfellas!*"

Hey, I don't judge people, but just know there are plenty of "bad" guys walking around in suits and ties just blending in. Make no mistake about it, bad guys are everywhere! You just have to look a little closer.

OK, just in case you're wondering, the subject is still Nashville, Opie, and "The Way It Worked." Trust me...

These same "party people" always say if there's anything they can ever do for me, all I have to do is *ask*. Hey, I might be a little naïve, but I'm not stupid! I saw *The Godfather*. I'm not asking for any favors, 'cause once you're *in*, you're *in* – you know what I mean? It's like that old Groucho Marx joke, "I wouldn't belong to any organization that would have me as a member!"

Even so, every now and then I'll get a phone call from a "member" asking me if I need anything. One day, I even received a gift without asking for it.

"Hey, Bobby," the familiar voice on the other end of the phone greeted me, "Do you like seafood?"

"Why, yes I do," I answered with a laugh.

"Well, go take a look outside your front door."

After hanging up the phone I opened the front door, and much to my surprise, I found a crate of fresh lobsters, clams, fish and oysters. Now personally, I *hate* oysters, but you know what? Who cares! Like I'm going to tell them that!

HOW IT WORKED

So, a few weeks after I get back from Nashville, I was walking down the street in New York City when I run into one of these so-called "bad" guys. There's a saying, "Big shots are just little shots that keep shooting!" Which must be why this particular guy considered me a big shot, because why else

56

would he ask, "Bobby, is there anything I can help you with?"

Trying to keep the panic inside my head about whether asking him for help will count as an I.O.U., I decided to throw caution into the wind and go for it. Maybe all I'll have to do is wear a black shirt with a white tie or buy a pinkie ring! I could handle a little quid pro quo! So I told my "member" friend the whole Tennessee Tale – all about Opie, the waitress, *everything*. I closed the story with how this guy still owes me money.

"Bobby, what would you like me to do about it?" he asked.

I was thinking to myself, *Why? Is there an order form? Let's see, bring me one club owner with a broken limb and I'll have two fingers on the side. No wait! Change that. Make that one finger and a severed head. I'm sorry, what's the special again? Oh, yeah right. OK, I'll have one torso floating in the bay with the picture of his nice-looking children pinned to his chest (I remember seeing this picture in his office!).*

Finally, I gave my answer, "How about get my money *and* an apology?"

Two days later, low and behold, my missing check arrived via FedEx and a few hours after that, I got a phone call. I listened as a very nervous Opie apologized for his behavior, while I don't say too much in response. To be honest, this is where the whole thing should end – you know, accept his apology and let him off the hook, *but that would be way too easy*! Besides, he deserved a little more payback than that. So, I told him what a poor example I think he's setting for the boys who work for him and his own male children by the horrible way he treats women – namely, that poor waitress! I then told him how disgusting he acted in his office when I came in for my check, playing Mr. Big Shot with his two cronies. It was here, in the middle of his second apology, that he told me how surprised he was that I knew the guy from Nashville that I did. Actually, I was just as surprised as he was. I'd run into the guy in New York City!

"Are you crazy?" Mr. Nashville had said to Opie. "You do know who the people are that Bobby knows, right? Pay the man his money!"

I'm pretty sure it was during *that* phone conversation that Opie's butt closed up. After retrieving his underwear and not passing Go, he called me to try and make amends.

Not wanting to prolong his agony any longer, I cut off the rest of his apology and casually asked, "How long have you been in this business?"

"Eighteen years," he replied.

"I think that's long enough. Don't you?"

CLICK!

About three months later, I got a call from my agent, "Bobby, do me a favor, call it off with this guy in Nashville."

"Call what off?" I asked.

My agent went on to explain that after Opie sent me my check, he was still paranoid. He was constantly looking over his shoulder – having bus boys start his car, waitresses take the first bite of his food, stuff like that. Apparently, things only went south from there and I heard through some comic friends that he went a little nuts, sold the club and left the business for good! He's now working for his wife's parents. See, every dog has his day!

WHY IT WILL ALWAYS WORK

Once again, this chain of events showed me without a shadow of doubt that what goes around DOES come around... *eventually*. Which is to say, as long as you're putting "good stuff" out there the Right Way, it will always come back to you when you need it most; but the real lesson here is when you put "bad stuff" out there, it will always come back to bite you in the ass.

Daniel Tosh and Bobby at The Comedy & Magic Club, Hermosa Beach, California. "Tosh.O... Bobby.Uh-Oh."

Chapter 5
CHILDREN

WE WERE GOING TO GET RID OF OUR KIDS BECAUSE THE DOG WAS ALLERGIC!

I was in the kitchen with the girls the other day and suddenly got a terrible headache, so I picked up the bottle of aspirin that's always on the windowsill. That's the first time I ever noticed "Keep Away From Children" on the label. I thought that was a good idea, so I swallowed two and went to my office over the garage – but it didn't work, they found me. Even more ironic is the fact that, until I was a father, I hadn't realized children are the reason aspirin was invented in the first place!

In all honesty, there's a part of me that thinks we should go back to beating our children (*Please don't! Comedic license here.)* Wait, I just heard Jill say, "Bobby, you're an asshole!" This is true from time to time, but entirely beside the point. Although admittedly, if we *did* beat our kids, I guess there'd be no need for my "look both ways down a one-way street" lesson plan – now would there?

I want to reassure anyone who's reading this – I *do not* and have *never* beaten either of my children. They truly are the loves of my life. Please, no anonymous child services tip-off calls needed here!

OUR FIRST BORN

Hallie is your typical twenty-something young woman. Now, if you've lived through the "maturing" of your own sweet, darling little girl, you will totally understand what I'm about to say. If your daughter hasn't yet reached those teen years, this is your PSA. Also, in no way do I claim to speak for other parents; however, I'm willing to bet a pair of Giorgio

Brutini shoes that I'm not alone on this one. Does God give you one kid who's a little fucked up? I can hear my father saying, "Yes. Yes, he does." Don't get me wrong. I love both my girls so much I just want to hug their hearts. But at other times – and *believe* me, there are times – I want to ask, "Do you need help packing?" There's a reason why some animals eat their young!

On the other hand, Jill says, "You have to love them all the same. They're all little gifts from God." No, they're not! More than once I've broached Jill about changing Hallie's name to Lucifer. She asks me questions like, "Daddy, are we rich?" I answer, "You're not! But I'm doing OK!" The music she listens to, this hip-hop stuff – *I'll take you to the candy shop/I'll let you lick the lollipop!* In my head I'm hearing, *All the leaves are brown and the sky is gray...* (another senior moment) I'm sure when I listened to The Doors, *my* father heard Glenn Miller!

Make no mistake about it – Hallie is a light in my life. She's beautiful like her mother, mischievous like her father, but naïve as hell! She's also too timid to stand up for herself with some of her friends, which causes her to go along with them even when she doesn't really want to. Her lack of assertiveness to avoid being taken advantage of is matched only by her tenacity to stick to a wrong decision – no matter how *wrong* that decision is! OK, time to roll up my sleeves and get to work – she's the one to keep my eye on!

They (again, I don't know who *they* are!) tell us our kids, around the age of thirteen, will board that spaceship to the inner-limits of their hormonal frontier, which coincidently is the outer limits of our patience! But fear not, *they* also tell us our kids have a round-trip ticket! Well, guess what? Hallie is in her twenties now and we're *still* waiting for her final re-entry! Although I will say her appearance more closely resembles the rest of us human beings these days and so does her speech. The music? Not so much!

Have we run the whole gamut with this child? You bet we have! Including, but not limited to, dabbling in recreational drugs, the mother-daughter dance of dominance, the criminal

61

boyfriend, the tattoos (I'm old school – you never put a bumper sticker on a Bentley!). She's changed universities *almost* as many times as she's changed her major.

Recently, she stopped by the space station (en route to yet another new university), so I took this opportunity to give her an honest assessment of who she was becoming. I told her, "You're turning out to embody everything in a person that I didn't like when I was growing up!"

See, we all have to learn about life our own way, and then live with our choices (and consequences). Through trial and error we discover the people we want to associate with, find the relationships we want to continue and who we want to become. I accept that my role as a parent is to guide my children and hopefully set the best example I can. But now that Hallie is an adult, it's her choice which life path she wishes to pursue. I can lead a horse to water and sit on its head to make it drink, but ultimately it has to be the horse's decision to swallow or spit!

Did I just compare my beautiful daughter to a horse?

I love Hallie with all my heart and I know she will always be an integral and important part of our lives, but God, really? You could have at least *mentioned* it wasn't going to be easy! Watch, she'll end up being a great female comedian!

ANGEL WITH A CLIPPED WING

When our second child, Madison (Maddie) Greer Collins, was born, Jill knew right away something was wrong – the baby didn't cry. She was non-responsive and lethargic. That was because Maddie was born with what they call "a disorder of the 23rd chromosome of an unknown origin." Translated to English – she doesn't walk very well and has never spoken a word. Although, as I've pointed out earlier, to me she speaks volumes! In her first three years alone she had at least thirty seizures (she eventually grew out of them), followed by three back operations, a constant schedule of therapies and too many hospital and doctor office visits to count. This sweet new soul set us on a different path indeed!

A few months after she was born, I remember sitting with my wife in a doctor's office and the doctor telling us Maddie's life expectancy was about ten years. He also told us we might want to consider placing her in a facility. My immediate response was, "It's OK! She's beautiful and she's ours!" I didn't care if she was just an arm – it was our arm and a perfect one at that! Besides, I thought who the hell was this doctor to know what she had in her? He didn't know me or Jill or anything about the family she would be going home to! He didn't know God's plan for this angel. Doctors – we need them, but come on! It's not a perfect science, so watch out for the white coats! I had just started to make my position very clear to the doctor, when Jill kicked me in the shin. Needless to say, we left *that* doctor's office and never returned.

Another doctor told us the parents of special needs children split up at a rate of 72%! Once I heard this, my mind was bombarded with questions... *Are we strong enough to handle this? Will Jill and I stay together? Can we give Madison what she needs from life?* But above all*, Why me? What did I do wrong? What's the karma at play here?* Well, it turned out, it's what I did right! Little did I know at the time that this perfect child would be the glue that keeps us a close and loving family.

To us, Maddie is perfect! I love this kid so much! I tear up just talking about her. Whenever I have a bad day or find myself worrying too much, the mere thought of her makes everything else just melt away.

Maddie's world has become our world. She sees everything through a different lens – a *wider* angle – and her world is infinitely more open. Because of this, our family's world is now bigger, fuller, brighter. It's a world of love, without judgments and regrets. We live a life filled with fun, laughter, tears, adventure, hope and peace. We have become impervious to the pitying looks, the well-intentioned, yet clumsy apologies from other people, the obvious turning away and the hushed comments. None of it matters!

Recently, my sister said to me, "When you were little, I

never thought you'd turn out to be such a *great dad*!" At first, I thought this was some sort of backhanded compliment, like she meant that I was such an asshole when I was younger that she's flabbergasted I turned out to be even a good dad! After all, how many times does your sister really give you an honest-to-goodness compliment? But when I realized she was being genuine, *it hit me like a rock*: if I didn't have Maddie in my life, I don't know that my sister would've been able to say that.

Because of Maddie, I'm always doing what needs to be done; including working hard to pay for her ongoing medical treatments. I also recognize that having a non-traditional career, with its travel commitments and off-hours, has sometimes left Jill to shoulder the day-to-day parenting responsibilities. This is why, now that I am in a position to do so, I make it a priority to set up my schedule so I have consecutive days at home with my family. I strive at all times to be more than just a paycheck, not because I *have* to, but because Maddie makes me *want* to be a better parent – to be a great dad! She's shown me how to thankfully and heartily enjoy my time on this big blue marble (however long that may be), along with the importance of prayer and the rewards of going places and meeting new people. Without the benefit of my own "Madison Greer Collins" telescope, I strongly suspect that might not be the case. And so it is with every part of my being that I, like so many other parents with special needs kids say, "Every family should be blessed with a special child!"

Jill and I both believe firmly in including Maddie in every experience "typical" families do, especially theater. I think that's because somewhere inside of me I'm still holding out hope that one day she's going to snap out of it and turn to me and say, "Thanks Dad for taking me to the theater! I've always loved it!"

In any event, we continue to frequent Broadway and once, while sitting in the front row of the Broadhurst Theater to see *Les Misérables* (it's not that we're hoity-toity front row *theatah* types, it's just that Maddie always reaches out and pulls the hair of the person sitting in front of her), during the most poignant moment of the musical, where half the audience is crying, Maddie lets out this bloodcurdling, set-your-hair-on-fire scream! You could see the shock and terror on the faces of the actors. I think half the audience expected Jean Valjean to call out, "Who just died?" I'm horrified! But what can I do? With lightning-fast comedic timing, I turn to the guy behind me and with *exaggerated* movement, I put my finger to my lips and give him a long, make a librarian proud – "Sssssshhhhh!" The look on this poor guy's face was priceless! He wanted to scream, "It wasn't me!" Laughing softly, Jill turned to me and said, "And THAT is why I married you."

In life, you have to deal with whatever comes up. All you can do is handle it and move on. Although, just remember, there's no law that says you can't have some fun with it along the way.

Today, Madison is a healthy, personable, funny, eighteen-year-old wonder, and I'm still determined to give her everything I can – no matter what it takes!

*HUMILITY IS NOT THINKING LESS OF YOURSELF,
IT'S THINKING OF YOURSELF LESS.*

—Rick Warren

From time to time, other comics ask me why I take certain jobs – jobs they feel are beneath my stature. "It's simple," I respond. "When you have a special needs child, you do *whatever* it takes to help pay for that extra pair of hands." Money doesn't discriminate; people do! I look back at some of the jobs I've taken over the years and I can't help but smile.

To that point, a gentleman recently came over to me after a theater performance and said, "I remember seeing you at a pie place in California" (it was Marie Callender's Comedy Night). I blushed when he told me this because I remember in addition to my small performance pay there was a bonus – *a free banana cream pie* – that I made sure I brought home for Maddie. Like I said, from day one, I've embraced this angel with a clipped wing and I'll always do what I can to make her life richer!

I always thought my heart was open, but it wasn't until Maddie came along that the doors to my heart swung completely wide open. In addition, I've learned (OK, so I'm still in the learning phase) patience, which has never been my strong suit. Case in point, Jill still hits me on the arm for honking at cars when we drive.

"Bobby, this is California! You're not in New York! We don't do that here!"

"But this idiot doesn't know how to drive!"

Or when we're out mingling with other people at an event and someone says, "Hey, Bobby. Did you see *Dancing with the Stars* the other night?" My response, "You should get a small room in your house and hang yourself! You're taking up space on the planet!" Again, Jill bops me or gives me the *maloik* – you know, the Italian "evil eye."

I guess, what Maddie has really taught me is to take a deep breath, slow down and simply follow the signs and go with the flow.

I've always heard people say that God has a plan and "all things happen for a reason;" that there's a method to the madness we live in and if you stick around long enough, the signs will present themselves. To be honest, I always wanted to believe this and *now* I do.

Our special angel Maddie had reached the age where we felt summer camp would be beneficial to her development. We didn't know of any special camps in California. We looked and looked, but couldn't find anything. Of course, our first criterion was to find a place with qualified personnel that were equipped to handle her special needs. On top of that, we had the usual parental concerns: *Will they take care of her? Will she eat right? Will she get cold at night? Will someone be there if she wakes up?*

By this time, my brother Tommy was retired from teaching and dealing with some health problems of his own, but since we had maintained a brotherly relationship, and he had an educational background, I called him to ask if he knew of a camp or had any suggestions. And guess what he suggested? Camp Jabberwocky. The same camp he'd worked

66

at many years ago. He told me he still had some connections with the camp and could get Maddie in, but cautioned, "Keep in mind, it's all the way across the country on Martha's Vineyard." When Jill and I spoke about it, I told her the story of visiting Tommy all those years ago and about giving Ronny a piggyback ride down to the lake.

After much discussion and trepidation, we packed Maddie up, flew with her to Massachusetts and checked into a summer motel (off-season, $49 dollars... in-season, $280 a night! *Location, location, location*). The first day we took her to camp, low and behold, sitting right there on the porch was none other than Ronny – now a sixty-seven year old man. When Ronny sees me, he comes running over, his arms and legs still flailing all over the place, and says, "I remember you! You're Tommy's brother! You gave me a piggyback ride down to the lake!" Wiping away tears, I reached out and gave Ronny a big hug. I then introduced him to Maddie.

In the years since, Ronny has always made it a point to welcome Maddie back to camp and make her feel at home. Unfortunately, Ronny passed away not too long ago. But you see, there is a plan and I was lucky to be part of it. I made my way back to Camp Jabberwocky, which was the right place for Madison. Thank God!

WHAT YOU PUT INTO A CHILD IS WHAT YOU GET OUT

When I was a kid, the news was on at 6 o'clock at night and if you missed it – see you tomorrow night! Today, it's on 24 hours a day. Children today are literally having the life scared out of them! Our society is in the middle of a full-blown audio and visual overload. We're *all* getting way too much information as it's happening, minute-by-minute, even if it's not important. You have to understand, I don't need to know that the Pope burped at 9:17 this morning or the tornado that hit Alabama is spreading – with every channel showing the same destroyed trailer park from a different angle – or that a tsunami is about to hit our shores here in Santa Monica,

California (which by the way, turned out to be about as exciting as farting in the bathtub) – just ripples! But hey, every news channel in town ran the same live coverage (every 15 minutes) showing all the people lined up down on the pier staring out into nothing. Does the saying "get a life" mean anything to you?

But the barrage never stops! And that's the problem. There's always something to scare the crap out of us – a nuclear meltdown in Japan, civil unrest in the Middle East (they all want the jeans!), North Korea and South Korea almost going to war. Then there's the flip-side of that fear (and to help keep us calm), the media fills our heads with absolute nonsense: Arnold and Maria broke up because he had a love child with their maid, Charlie Sheen is hanging out on one of the rings of Saturn, a housewife from Orange County just lost a boob, Kim Kardashian's X-ray showed there IS actually a marble rolling around inside her head. The lunacy never ends!

The fact is, we're living in a sad world with our feet firmly resting on a mad little planet, which makes it that much more difficult for the rest of us who are trying to raise healthy, kind, thoughtful and respectful human beings who'll eventually take over for us when we're gone. But you know what? We can't leave the job to others! We simply have no choice! We have to set the examples for our children – they're too important!

Here's another contributing facet: it dawned on me not too long ago that Jill and I drove our kids everywhere. It's a way of life now for parents now. A "play date" used to be when the neighborhood moms would walk their toddlers to the playground (in my case, a playground was only a sandbox in the common area of the apartments) so they could play while the moms got some much needed adult social time. Today, a "play date" means anytime your kid wants to do anything with someone else's kid, you have to drive them somewhere, drop them off, pick them up and make sure they're looked after. Then there's the whole arrival/departure interrogation, "Do you have money?" "Did you bring a sweater?"

"Did you eat anything?" "Were her parents nice to you?" Put a needle in my eye! We're bringing up a generation of weenies! What are they going to be prepared for in life? Knitting? And the medical community wonders why one out of every three kids is obese? Duh! They never fucking walk! Our kids are also told to watch out for predators on every corner, always have a "buddy" and never go *anywhere* without their cell phone. Hallie called Jill the other day to ask if dinner was ready... from her bedroom upstairs! They can't even go to church anymore because they fear Father Pedophile might give them his secret spiritual lift! On top of that, everything is blamed on al-Qaida. I asked Hallie recently, "Why are you failing English?" Her reply, "al-Qaida." If we listen to our so-called spineless leaders, al-Qaida is lurking behind every bush, so *be very fearful*. I didn't realize how much all this fear had seeped in until I recently took a bad spill skiing. When Jill finally pulled me out of the trees, she asked, "What the hell happened?" Without thinking, I screamed, "al-Qaida!"

It's no wonder our kids are nervous overeaters. I'm surprised they're not wearing flak jackets and carrying missile detectors in their backpacks!

I remember one day shortly after September 11th, Hallie (she was ten years old at the time) looked up at me with her big beautiful eyes and asked, "Daddy are we going to die?" I answered, "Oh no, my angel. We're just going through a correction in life. We have to go through this in order to get to a better place."

Despite my answer, my heart was heavy, but my resolve was even stronger. Have we arrived at that better place yet? No, we haven't, but I think we're getting closer. My goal then is still my goal now – to lighten the load for others and deflate the bubble of fear by replacing it with the helium of laughter! I have to stand on stage and tell people the truth, so that when the government comes up with another *brilliant* display of ineptitude, like every home should have one room duct taped with plastic sheeting so nothing can escape, I must shout, "Have you ever farted in your pajamas? It always gets out!" Remember, "The truth shall set you free!" and in some cases "Air you out!"

Our children are our future, so let's leave this place better then we found it. *Take responsibility.* Love your children, but understand your job is to be a parent, not a pocketbook. You have to lead by example. You can't be a bystander or a "buddy" – it's your duty to keep them from harm's way, and that requires that YOU set limits and rules and administer consequences. For at least 18 years, you have the (*gasp!)* right to tell them what they can and cannot do in order to claim the privilege of producing thoughtful, caring, socially conscious, and productive human beings.

Just keep an industrial bottle of aspirin handy and you'll get through it!

ADDENDUM

Since the completion of this chapter, I was honored to speak at my daughter's 18th birthday party. Normally at private functions, I give a personalized stand-up performance. However, in this case, because this was such a personal, near-to-my-heart gathering, I wrote and delivered... a poem (the only one I've ever written).

I hesitated about including this in the book because truthfully, I don't want anyone to think for one second I consider myself a poet. However, because I have been approached by many of those in attendance that night asking for a copy, I decided to share it here.

I HAVE A VOICE

Eighteen years ago, God sent me on a special mission
to spend some time with two people.
Not just any two people – two people who
I was told
really needed me
to teach them a few things.

70

In turn, they would care for and love me unconditionally!
Boy did *I* have my hands full.
One of these people, the Dad
let me tell you, for *this* one I really had to roll up my sleeves
is loud and impatient!
Yet at the same time, he's loving and fun to be around.
He dances, sings, builds bonfires and *always* laughs.
He takes me in the car with him and lets me sit in the front seat!
When people stare, he runs interference
to make me feel comfortable and accepted.
Secretly, *I think he's doing it for himself as much as he's doing it for me.*
But no matter
because he's fun to watch
and I find him entertaining and amusing
as he helps me be everything I can be.
Dad is my *protector*.
I HAVE A VOICE
Now the other one is the Mom. She's really pretty and kind.
She does things for me (and other people)
without ever thinking of herself.
She is loving and fun to be around.
Here's another secret
I take advantage of her sometimes by being demanding
Like when I give her one of my "Hey I'm talking to you!" looks
she knows exactly what it means and gives me her attention.
Or if I let her know, "Yo, Momma – I'm hungry and could ya
change my drawers right about now?"
She goes into full Mom mode.
Mom worries about me all the time.
She's constantly on the front line for me,
whether it's going to school, traveling, eating or sleeping.
She's always vigilant (even militant if need be)
when it comes to maintaining my health.
She always makes sure I'm warm and dressed properly
and she's almost obsessed about brushing my teeth clean!
She's the first to fight my battles – all my battles
in the school, the hospital, the court,

or just out for a walk.
I've thanked God many times for this family
but especially for sending me to Her!
Mom is my *life warrior*.
I HAVE A VOICE
God selects some of us to be examples for everyone else.
Just because someone looks or sounds different
it does not mean they're any less!
Look around at your own lives.
We all need examples to show us the right path
to continue on our own journeys.
I'm eighteen years now with these two.
We're doing OK
we all have to work a little harder
especially the LOUD ONE
but we will all get there!
My name is Madison Greer Collins and
I HAVE A VOICE

My Angel - Madison

Chapter 6
A FRIEND IN NEED IS A FRIEND INDEED

I know a lot of people who call themselves my friend, so I let them, even though some of them don't have a clue as to what a friend is or how friendship works. Why? Because I've found that letting them think we're friends makes them feel better about who they are or where they are in their own journey. I've also found that some of these so-called friends do it to simply show off (sad, but true) to their friends that they know me. They want to play Big Shot, so again, I let them, as long as they're not being a dick about it – high-fives and "Wassup's?" all around!

But to those people who actually *are* my friends, I'm a good friend. I don't take friendship lightly, and I expect others to do the same. There have been many times in my life that someone who I thought was a good friend turned out not to be and let me tell you, *that* hurt. But ultimately, I learned the only people I really need in my life are the ones that need me in theirs... and for the right reasons!

Growing up, every neighborhood (mine included) had its own "gang" (think *Little Rascals*.) In the summer, we ruled the streets, playing games like Ringolevio or Red Light, Green Light, where you had to scream out, "Five-Ten, You're One of My Men!" when you got caught.

How many people do you still know from your childhood?

I still know and love my childhood friend, Alan. We went our separate ways for a while before coming full circle. He now also lives in California (near me) and I'm proud to say that I'm the godfather to his kids. We talk every day, and I can always feel that bond from the old neighborhood. We also tend to look at life the same way. For one thing, Jill says, "You're both frugal guys," which, as she reminds me, is her *polite* word for cheap! Hey, when you grow up poor, you develop a more discerning eye when it comes to *want* versus *need*. While Alan

74

also may be frugal with his money, he wears his heart on his sleeve and you know what? It's *pure* gold.

There were other kids from the old neighborhood who weren't as lucky as Alan and me. One of our other childhood buddies was a guy named David Kaufman. David taught us how to dance and gave us a safe place to hang out after school. His mother Dottie was the kindest woman in the world, and his stepfather, Sol, would drive us anywhere we wanted to go, no questions asked. Ahh, the good old days. I can close my eyes right now and still see the clothes I wore, the smile on my face, the games we played and the disappointment I felt when my mother called me home from David's house for dinner. Unfortunately, it would be a long time before I saw David again.

They say life is made up of the choices we make. I was in eighth grade when we moved to New Hyde Park, Long Island. I missed my old friends at first, but there were new adventures waiting for me. I adapted pretty quickly, but it was real hard on my brother Roy. He kept running back to the old neighborhood to hang out with his cronies. He just didn't see that what we were leaving was now over and it was time to turn the page and move in another direction – a better direction! On Long Island, we had a house, a garage, a driveway, a lawn, a pool table and our own rooms. I felt like a Rockefeller! I made new friends, played basketball, joined clubs – I thought it was great! The downside was I eventually lost touch with many of my friends from the old neighborhood, but those memories are etched into my heart forever. My journey had just taken a different turn.

As I've said, after high school, my next stop was the University of Buffalo, where Alan was my roommate. Four years later, after freezing my ass off, I came back home looking to buy some time and find a direction. Remember, before I was a comedian full-time, I had a number of other jobs: I was a high-school substitute teacher, a steel salesman before I became a jewelry entrepreneur, and finally, a Garmento, a Calvin Klein executive. It was around my Calvin Klein stint that I'd heard David had gotten married and had a couple of kids. Which reminded me of the fact that when you fall out of touch with most people from your youth, it's certainly not on purpose – it's just that life happens and people move in different directions.

Jumping ahead to November 1992, I'm working and living in New York City, appearing mostly at the comedy club *Caroline's* (when I first started there it was called only *Caroline's* and it was located on 28th Street & 8th Avenue; eventually it relocated to the heart of the theater district and is now called *Caroline's On Broadway*). It was (and still is) a headliner club for the most recognized names in comedy.

When you work the clubs, you get to know the staff, and at that time, the doorman at *Caroline's* was a struggling actor who also happened to be named Bobby. Bobby was a native New Yorker, with a well-developed "forgetaboutit" attitude, but deep down he was a good guy with a good heart (he later became a regular on the HBO show *The Sopranos*). One night, Bobby mentioned to me that a homeless man was hanging around the block asking about me. "No problem," I told him. "I don't discriminate! I have fans at all caste levels!"

By this time, I'd heard all the rumors that David had lost his family due to drugs and was living on the street. I remember my first thought was this homeless man might be David, so I immediately ran around the block looking for him, but I couldn't find him. I had this funny feeling that David was watching me the whole time, but just didn't want to be found... *you just know.*

A few years later, the night before Thanksgiving – a freeze-your-nose-hair-stiff kind of cold night – my family and I were walking down Fifth Avenue on our way back to our hotel. I'd heard from David's mother that he sometimes slept in a church entrance somewhere in Manhattan, but she had no idea where. As my family and I walked down Fifth Avenue on this frigid night, I felt something strange and slowed up. A little ways up the street, I could see a church on 56th Street and Fifth Avenue with about fifteen cardboard boxes pushed together on the steps. I thought how sad it was for these people. Here it was a night too cold to even *be* outside and they were *sleeping* outside. I counted my blessings and then hurried everyone along in order to reach the warmth of our hotel room as quickly as possible. But just before we reached 56th Street, I stopped across from the church and yelled out, "David Kaufman!"

"Who's that?" a faint voice shouted back.

"Bobby Collins!"

Next thing I know, a shadow of a man popped his head out from one of the cardboard boxes and without thinking, I stepped out into the street toward him, "Jill! It's him! Come on! Look, it's David!"

Not wanting to trust the kindness of New York City traffic, Jill redirected the girls to an actual crosswalk. When they reach me on the other side of the street, a shocked (and probably a little frightened) Hallie grabbed my hand. "Daddy? Do *you* know him?"

As David approached us, he turned to the other box people and with unrestrained Ed McMahon-like exuberance delivered what I consider to be the most fervent, heart-felt, stage introduction I ever or *will* ever receive, "Hey people! This is Bobby Collins! A famous comedian! And my friend!"

I was humbled by David's words and after we hugged for a long time, I introduced him to my family. He was missing a bunch of teeth and you could see the devastating toll drugs and the elements had taken on him – his hair was matted and his clothes all tattered and torn. As I looked deeper into his eyes, I could also see the pain buried deep within him. But for a brief moment, we were both fresh-faced kids again, standing in front of the long mirror in his bedroom dancing under his instructions, "OK, make like you're threading a needle. That's it! Now, move your arms!"

I thanked David for all of the support and kindness he gave me as a kid – teaching me about girls, how to dance, even giving me a new shirt when I needed it. I told him it was an honor and privilege to know him and I was grateful I had the chance to introduce him to my family. When I finished, everyone had tears running down their cheeks.

I then invited David to join us for Thanksgiving dinner

at Carmine's (a well-known New York City Italian restaurant) and while he said he'd try to make it, I knew he wouldn't. I hugged him goodbye, and so as not to embarrass him, I discreetly slipped a $50 bill into his pocket (it's all I had!). Jill held me tight that night and to this day Hallie still brings up the time we ran into my old friend David in the freezing cold on Fifth Avenue. Lessons come in different ways, now don't they?

I haven't seen David again since that night, but his mother Dottie called me sometime later and thanked me for being so kind to him when I saw him on the street. She expressed how proud he was of me, how much it meant for him to meet my family and for what I said to him. She also told me he was too embarrassed to go to Thanksgiving dinner, but he appreciated the offer. I thanked her for the call and also for sharing her son with me. It must be hard on a mother to know that one of her babies is living on the street (I count my blessings every day).

Here's a footnote to the David story and how life comes full circle: I was teaching a one- night course on comedy at the Learning Annex (a private outfit that promotes cultural interests in New York City) to about seventy-five people, all of whom had signed up for the three-hour course for $50. The whole time leading up to this night, I was trying to figure out how in the world you teach the art of comedy to a group of strangers in just three hours! Well, it turns out my anxiety was for nothing. *After four and a half hours*, the class ended and I was feeling great for being able to share my knowledge with others. It was fun, entertaining and the time flew by. I had the energy of ten men! It also brought back my old teaching abilities, and I'm not embarrassed to tell you, I patted myself on the back for the class going so well.

One young guy, who looked to be in his late twenties, stuck around longer than the rest of the gawkers, waiting until everyone else left before approaching me cautiously and introducing himself, "Hi. I know we don't know each other, but I think you might know my dad. My name is Josh Kaufman." It was David's son!

Josh went on to tell me that even though he was estranged from his father for years, he still remembered how he always talked about me. I sensed all the rage, hurt, disappointment and feeling of abandonment in Josh when he talked about his father. After hanging around in the classroom for a while, I invited him to join me for coffee so we could talk some more. As we sat across from each other, I told him stories of what his father was like growing up and how we all eventually went our separate ways. In life, God deals the cards; it's how we play them that counts.

During this conversation, Josh confided in me that he wanted to pursue a career in comedy – *our bond was forming!* I went on to explain how to take the subjects from his own life, the ones that make him laugh and cry, and take a hard look at them so he can see where he made different choices than other people made. This way he would truly understand these choices and talk about them. I told him this might be tough to do at first, but it gets easier over time. Once you see things from this perspective, you realize things are happening for a reason, and that it's up to you to decide if you want to use them in your routine (or not). And since it's your own life, you get to decide whether you see things as positive or negative. I guess that's why we all have to pay our dues! *Growth means change.*

Everyone thinks his or her story is the worst. You talk to enough people and you begin to realize we *all* have a story. It's how we choose to read this story that defines who we are. Some people don't read at all, while others understand, change and grow from what happens to them.

Josh is married now and working as a comic traveling from city to city telling *his* story. And what a beautiful story it is! I don't know if he'll ever know his dad the same way I knew him – as the guy growing up with the kind heart and giving soul, a teacher and dancer. But hey, shit happens!

While we meet many people over the course of our lives who want to be friends for the right reasons, we also meet many people over the course of our lives who want to be friends for the wrong reasons. Every person brings something to the table, even if it's only pulling up a chair! So don't believe just because someone has been around since childhood, they will or *should* always be in your life. If you come to the realization that a friend can't (or won't) provide what you need, which should be to exemplify, support and enhance who you are or who you want to become *at this moment in your life* – you might need to make some changes. After all, time is relative; growth is essential. A true friend will not only make you feel better about yourself, they will make adjustments with you to ride out the ebbs and flows in order for the friendship to endure (speaking from personal experience, you can substitute the word *spouse* for *friend*). But even if someone doesn't stick around for the long haul, you should never forget the good times you had together. You simply need to keep the best and leave the rest!

As I said before, over the years I've been hurt by friends. As a result, those friendships fell away. Of course, when it happened, I immediately blamed myself (remember, I'm Catholic!).

Case in point, I had this one friend from college, Barry. Nice guy, lots of fun. After college, most of us went our separate ways trying to find out where we fit in this world, but Barry and I remained friends, and anytime I'd be in New York working, we'd get together. As a comic, you need these oases during your travels, where you can let your guard down and just be yourself.

My wife, Jill, is a very perceptive person. Whenever I mentioned Barry, she would tell me, "Bobby, don't you see? Barry is jealous of you." The truth is, I think I felt something, too, but I couldn't see it for what it was, or maybe I just didn't *want* to look deep enough. Either way, I felt close to him based upon our ties from the past. Well, one day, Barry calls me out of the blue and it was the strangest call. He had a business proposal he wanted to discuss with me. He wanted us to go into booking theaters together. We'd split all the costs, as well as all the profits (after my normal appearance fee was paid). I was quite taken aback by this because we'd never talked about business before. It was always just fun between us.

After listening to Barry, I informed him that I was in

the process of booking theaters on my own, using my own money. And even though I didn't want to come across as disingenuous, I said, "Honestly, Barry, why would I need you anyway? What are you bringing to the table?" He responded with such anger, almost to the point of being downright nasty, that I pulled the conversation back and suggested, "Let me think about it some more and I'll give you a call later." Truth is, normally I would've fired back with both guns blazing at *anyone* who talked to me that way, but I was so taken aback that it was Barry that my ass closed up like a napkin holder!

After absorbing the whole conversation and weighing the pros and cons, I called him back and relayed my feelings. I mentioned how many friendships fall by the wayside when business and money come into play and I didn't want to see this happen to ours. So I thanked him for the offer, but let him know it would be best if we kept our relationship on a friendship-only basis. His response was venomous. He yelled into the phone, "Fine! But don't call me when you really need me!" CLICK! I was so confused and pissed off by his behavior that I didn't know what to do,

Once I had some time to calm down, I rationalized in my head that maybe he's going through a rough patch with his wife or business and that he'll call back in a day or two. Because you know how it is – after you've had some time to think about things, you realize you may have said things to someone you didn't really mean. I'm a firm believer in taking responsibility for one's own self and actions, and if the situation were reversed, I know I would've called Barry back to apologize, no doubt making some sort of self-deprecating comment like, "Sorry about the other day. I guess I threw another surprise party in my head without telling anyone." But you know what? Barry never called me back... and I never called him either.

This now brings me to my friend Paula (don't worry, this all gets tied together). I've known Paula for over twenty years. We're so close that not only do I think of her as Maddie's godmother, I consider her an extension of our family, as well. The good thing is Jill understands Paula, even though from time-to-time Paula has made comments implying she knows me better than Jill does (based on the fact she's known me longer). Had the tables been turned, I don't think I'd be as understanding as Jill if another man implied he knew her better than I did, but Jill is like that – she sees Paula for who she is: a lonely middle-aged woman who's afraid of commitment and has no family in California. So even though Jill could choose to see Paula as a threat, she's never pushed her away, although she did tell me, "You just don't want to *look,* Bobby. That girl loves you." Even Hallie said to me, "Daddy, if anything ever happened to Mommy, Paula would be right at our door."

As you now know, I don't like to see these things about people who are close to me. I mean, how long did it take with Barry? So I ignored my family's comments and continued to treat Paula the same way I always did – as an old friend. Except, I have to be honest, Jill and Halle's observations did take a foothold in the back of my mind.

One day, not too long after Jill's comment, Paula and I were having lunch when I said to her seemingly out of nowhere, "I know there will be a time when I really need you and you won't be there for me." I still have no idea where this came from; it just sort of spilled out of my mouth While I'm sure Paula was as shocked to hear this as I was to say it, we never actually spoke about it, even though I never forgot I was the one who said it.

To make a long story even longer, Paula went through a tough divorce with her husband and she asked me to step in. I didn't hesitate for a second and went as far as to hide her in our house to protect her, which once again left me holding the bag.

Random thought here – I never really understood that saying "left holding the bag." It's not clear to me. Is one left holding a tea bag? Their own balls? Or what? Is it just a way of saying everything turned out for the better *except* for the person who got sucked into something they didn't want to be involved with in the first place! Sorry, but this "left holding the bag" thing has always bothered me. Whatever the definition, in this case, it meant I was the one left holding an imaginary bag filled with other people's (Paula and what's-his-name's) issues.

Anyway, to continue, I was away performing in Atlantic City for a few days. Now, Atlantic City, there's a real shithole! All these old hotels badly in need of renovations, built right on the Atlantic Ocean, where fish wash up on the shore carrying IV bottles. It always looks to me like a pirate ship landed there – all these people with hands and limbs missing! Just to keep sane, I walk around the place challenging strangers to fights, "Arrghh! On guard, matey." A friend at the hotel where I was working asked, "Bobby, where's the men's room?" I told him, "Look at the carpet! Just piss anywhere you want!"

I think we've all stayed in that hotel where you didn't want to touch *anything*; where you go to bed at night with your hands in the air saying to yourself, "Could I get a black light and a CSI Unit in here?" There are more insurgents in Atlantic City than Iraq. I saw Osama bin Laden playing blackjack. No one cared!

To get back to our story, I'm all the way across the country doing these shows in Atlantic City when I received a phone call from Maddie's school. They explained to me they couldn't reach Jill to let her know Maddie has been spiking a fever and has been throwing up. DING! DING! DING! It's important to know that when our little Maddie gets sick, we go into high alert! Her wiring is different from ours. Her body temperature can reach 105° in the blink of an eye.

I hung up the phone with Maddie's school and immediately tried calling Jill myself, but I got nothing! Thinking as quickly as I could, I decided to call Paula. She lived only five blocks from our house and worked only about ten minutes away. Luckily, when I called her, she had just walked through her front door (which I was little surprised by), so I asked, "What are you doing home?"

She told me, "Bobby, I'm feeling sick, like I'm coming down with the flu."

GREAT! Timing is everything.

I told her about the phone call I just received and how I haven't been able to reach Jill. I asked if she could pick Maddie up and take her to our house.

"Bobby, I'm not feeling well," she told me again. "I just want to get into bed."

For the first time in my life, I was momentarily stunned silent. But that didn't last too long. As soon as I snapped back, my silence was replaced by unrestrained anger. I yelled into the phone, "I don't care if your arm is hanging off and blood is squirting all over the place! Get over to Maddie's school and pick her up right now!" While I'm sure Paula was shocked by my outburst, I didn't care. All I cared about is that she agreed to pick up Maddie.

When Jill finally called back a few minutes later, I brought her up to speed on everything, including the *red flag* I got on Paula. I was really hurt Paula didn't feel the same sense of urgency for Maddie that I did. I tried to rationalize her behavior by blaming it on the fact she never had children of her own, but actually I thought... *Here's someone who never learned the Golden Rule!* While it's true people often get wrapped up in their own world and sometimes have to be reminded about what's important – deep down, we all know! The difference is I would parachute from a Boeing 747 to help a friend if they needed me. Of course, when I told Jill about how hurt I was by Paula, she tried to smooth things over by saying, "Not everyone is like you. People have their own agendas."

The last straw with Paula came not too long after the whole situation with Maddie's school. I was scheduled to do a few shows in New York City over a long weekend and Jill asked if she could come with me so we could spend some time together.

"Bobby, it would be so nice if we could do this, just the two of us."

"I think that's a great idea," I told her. "I would love that."

You have to understand, because of our special needs angel, it's hard for Jill and me to get away, even for a night or two. We can't just leave Maddie alone in our house like we can with Hallie. We have to come up with a carefully constructed plan for her.

So, to get ready for the long weekend, Jill and I sat down and went through our usual roster of housesitters and babysitters to see who was available. Unfortunately, we couldn't find anyone to help us out over the busy weekend. Out of options, we called Paula, and when we got her on the phone, Jill – Goddess Artemis that she is when it comes to *all* things Madison – explained, "Maddie will have a caregiver at the house until nine each night and another aide will arrive each morning at six to get her ready for the day. All we really need you to do is sleep over to make sure everything goes smoothly."

While I didn't expect Paula to react as if she'd just won the lottery, I guess I was so relieved that we were able to get Maddie's care covered, I didn't notice her rather nonchalant, "OK, I'll stay over while you're gone." After all, she'd just opened the door to a weekend alone with my bride! This was going to be great – have fun, work, have some more fun and of course, shake-it-while-ya-make-it-'cause-there-'ain't-no-kids-to-break-it sex!

A week before the trip, I spoke to Paula again, but *this* time my radar definitely received a hit. There was something in her voice that made me wonder – *What's going on inside her head?* I will say this for Paula: she's always been pretty good at telling me how she feels. Remember, I make my living on a stage. I have honed and strengthened my natural perceptive and intuitive abilities by years of observing people. Call it a sixth sense, if you will. I can look out into an audience and *know* who I should speak to, who I should avoid, who's married and who shouldn't be, just by using my special ability. While other people make me use my sixth sense, Paula never has, which is something I've always appreciated. I'd much rather people tell me the information upfront that they think I don't want to hear, so I don't have to waste my time trying to figure it out.

I have to say, even knowing how Paula can be, I was surprised when she made it quite clear how she felt, telling me, "I'm coming over this weekend, but I just have to tell you, I hated babysitting when I was a kid. I'll do this for you and Jill this one time, but I don't want to do it anymore."

What I *should* have said back to her is, *Why the hell didn't you just say "No" in the first place?* At the same time, in my head, I was singing that song – *People Who Need People Are the Luckiest People in the World* - because I realized pretty quickly that if I actually said to her what I *should* have said, she would've immediately gotten defensive or freaked out on me. So, in my calmest voice possible, I told her, "Why don't you just come over so we can talk about this weekend some more?"

When Paula walked into the house, Jill and I were watching television with the kids. After a few minutes of harmless small talk, I brought up to Jill what Paula had said to me on the phone. OK, to be honest, I actually mimicked her voice when I repeated, "I'm only babysitting for you guys this one time. After this – no more!" Jill started laughing (in that Bobby's just screwing around laugh) when she heard this, but stopped when Paula blurted out rather awkwardly, "That's right, Jill. That's what I said. I meant it when I said it to Bobby over the phone and I mean it now. This is a onetime deal."

The next morning, I woke up early to find Jill lying in bed staring at the ceiling. I could see right away the disappointment and hurt on her face. As soon as she saw that my eyes were open, she announced, "I'm not going to New York with you this weekend. You go without me. I don't want someone looking after my children who doesn't want to be with them."

I knew there wasn't anything I could say or do to change her mind, and while it hurt me, it pained me even more to see the hurt Paula had caused (once again). Only this time, the hurt was to Jill, the same woman who ignored all the "one-up's" Paula thought she'd camouflaged (rather unsuccessfully) over the years. With one selfish "disclaimer," Paula had forced the retreat of my wife who extends herself – *to everyone* – in so many ways. So much so, I sometimes find myself getting upset with her generosity, particularly when it comes to money (don't forget, I'm cheap!).

The kicker to this story comes while I was in New York

that weekend. Paula called me and asked, "Are you upset with me?" I didn't respond at first and let her go on to say, "I've been feeling you very strong these last few days. This doesn't have anything to do with our friendship, does it?" See, people always know!

Her words "our friendship" somehow struck a nerve with me, turning out to be the catalyst that led to my pivotal thought – *Why have you been waiting so long to be honest with yourself?* Suddenly, I felt empowered and decisive about Paula. Not wanting to wait another second, I finally told her flat-out, "We can't be friends anymore." And just like that, it was over.

I soon realized ending a twenty-some-odd-year friendship was going to create a lot of questions, which meant I was going to have to come up with a lot of answers. Damn! Once again I'm left holding the bag!

Right on cue, the minute I walked into the house from New York, Jill asked, "What's up with you and Paula?" At the same time, Hallie was a little more direct, wanting to know, "Why aren't you and Paula friends anymore?" I explained to both of them as honestly and straightforward as I possibly could about what happened and why I decided to end the friendship. And while I didn't think I owed anyone else an explanation, apparently I was alone in my thinking, because even today mutual friends ask, "Bobby, twenty years is a lot of history just to toss away. Don't you think maybe you should at least talk to Paula?" My answer to them is always the same: "No, I *don't* need to talk to her." Enough said. Remember, actions always speak louder than words!

To finish out the Paula story, that day after hanging up the phone – essentially disconnecting from her completely even though I was feeling the strength from within about how I'd interpreted her words and behavior – I still was looking for some confirmation that my decision wasn't made based on anything I'd misconstrued. In my world, "Measure twice, cut once," doesn't just apply to wood! So, as a matter of course, I ran the whole thing by God. I do this at times so I don't confuse myself, or anyone else for that matter. After all, how irresponsible of me would it be to not check with a higher authority to make sure my actions were based on truth and not just what I *thought* was the truth? Once I finished explaining the whole situation to God, along with the feelings that led to my decision, I asked if He could give me a sign, an ANSWER as to whether ending my friendship with Paula was the right decision for the right reasons. I knew this was a selfish thing to ask, but I needed to do it so I could be at peace and just let it go.

After preparing in my hotel room for the show, and with Paula still strongly on my mind, I walked the eight minutes to *Caroline's On Broadway*. There, standing in front of the club, smiling like a Cheshire cat was an *undeniable* sign – my old friend Barry. *Hey, God, you're really good at this*, I thought. Seeing Barry didn't just make me happy; it made me walk a little taller and feel a little stronger. But most of all, it humbled me.

The first sentence out of his mouth was, "Your friendship in this life means more to me than anything else and I don't want to lose it." Without hesitation, I invited Barry into the club so we could talk in private. While I knew it would never be exactly the same between us, I also knew the hurt and disappointment that came from my friendship with Paula served as a guide so Barry and I could come full circle.

Everyone likes to fall under the column of friendship, but some people don't want to work for it.

Garry Shandling and Bobby at The Comedy & Magic Club. "Now the world knows...WE are the real men in black."

I got my answer from God that night, and I haven't looked back. Friendship is nothing to take lightly; it's something you need to work at. But the work doesn't have to be hard!

I have to be thankful for knowing the friends I've had in my lifetime – some old, some new and some who've shown by their actions to be above and beyond any spoken word. I respect the bond of friendship and continue to work each day at being the best friend I can possibly be, because it's true what *they* say (*they* certainly say a lot, don't *they!*): "To have a good friend, you have to be a good friend."

Chapter 7
DEFINE THE MOMENT OR THE MOMENT DEFINES YOU

I don't think this will come as surprise to anyone, but not everyone you encounter, even members of your own family, are always going to be nice to you... or even like you! Which is OK, because many times the feeling is mutual – in which case, it's just a matter of *Ob-La-Di, Ob-La-Da!*

However, there are times when someone you know and like will inadvertently say or do something you may not like, but they fall under the category of "shit happens." You merely chalk up whatever it is they do or say to a brain fart, understand there was no malicious intent, and simply extend an "Excuse you."

Next, you may have some people who knowingly say or do something to upset you because they believe *wholeheartedly* they are acting in *your* best interest. They're just crazy makers and we all have them (they're mostly family members!).

The problem as I see it are those people who, because they are jealous or envious or just plain mean, deliberately heave a monkey wrench into your life.

I'm talking about people whose goal (short or long term) is to try and control or manipulate you. In short, they fuck *you* over for their own selfish reasons! Which is why, before you write something off as mere happenstance, you first need to ask yourself if there's a motive behind what someone says or does. And if there is, whom does it benefit? You or them?

NEVER LET THEM SEE YOU SWEAT

Make no mistake about it – those types of people are not nice! That is why it's important to know not only *what* to

90

say to these people, but *how* to say it. First and foremost: Never give someone who wishes you ill will (either in words or actions) the satisfaction of knowing or even *thinking* they got to you. Malicious people take great pleasure in their convoluted facade of superiority!

If I allowed everyone who lobbed their maliciousness my way to think they actually got to me, I would curl up in a ball on the couch with my thumb up my ass feeling sorry for myself! This is all the more reason I felt it was important that my girls learned early on to identify and deal with those people, too. Because believe me, there's no more malicious species on the planet than a pack of pubescent girls!

When Hallie was twelve years old, she came home from school one day and found me in the den. Immediately, she went into a winding recitation about what she did that day, who was whose best friend, who had the coolest shoes, why she hated gym class and only momentarily stopped to ask, "Do we have any snacks?" Heading into the kitchen, she continued talking... about a lot of things! I don't remember everything she said, but I do remember her telling me something about a field trip on Friday. She then said with a mouthful of food, "A girl in my class asked me to make her a sandwich for lunch tomorrow." I'll admit I had sort of "zoned out" a little by then, somewhere around the time she was telling me what Susie had said when she heard what Tommy had told Ben after he talked with Tiffany. Really, the only "good dad" response I could think to give was, "Are you going to need money for the field trip?"

The next morning, I found Hallie in the kitchen making two sandwiches, so I asked her, "Who's the second sandwich for?"

"Don't you remember, Daddy? I told you yesterday. It's for a girl in my class."

Playing the afterschool recap through my head, I said, "Ah, I do remember there was something about a sandwich." That's when I recalled what she'd said about the girl. It became apparent that Hallie was convinced the girl was going hungry; that she didn't have the means to make or buy her own lunch.

While I admired that Hallie wanted to help this girl (there's a lot of Jill in this kid!), I also felt the school (or at least their teacher) should be made aware of the situation.

I finally said, "Oh, yeah... right. You're making a sandwich for what's-her-name."

"Alana," Hallie replied as she wrapped up the extra sandwich with double turkey, two types of cheese, all neatly placed on a fresh jumbo croissant. RED FLAG! I know Alana's family. They could afford to build a Subway sandwich shop in the school cafeteria if they wanted to! I also knew Alana was part of the "cool girls," so I couldn't help but smile a little at the whole situation. Here's my sweet little girl, with a heart as big as Texas, who just wants to be friends with everyone, naïvely thinking this double-decker deli delight was her *in* with the "cool girls."

I said to Hallie, "Sit down a minute. Let's talk about something." As we sat at our kitchen table, I explained to her that if fitting in means someone else is controlling you, *that's* not friendship. She understood right away and that day at school (sans the sandwich), she told Alana, "If you want me to be your friend, it has to be because you like me and not because you just think I'll do anything you tell me to do." Well, guess what? Alana apologized. Only after Hallie showed her confidence and never let Alana see her sweat, did they become (and have remained) friends.

YOU ARE A SLAVE TO NO ONE

Early in my career, I was booked at a comedy club in Mystic, Connecticut, for two shows on Friday night and two shows on Saturday night. With my signed contract for $5,000.00 ($1,250.00 per show) in hand and plane reservations made, I was ready to go! But little did I know the rug was about to be pulled out from under me. The night before the gig, I got a phone call from the booking agent, who told me the club owner was no longer willing to pay my full appearance fee. It was going to be *two thousand dollars* less! "Why?" I ask.

The booking agent says, "Sorry, take it or leave it."(Yeah, there are those types of agents out there – bad ones.) You have to understand, at this point in my career, every dime from my appearances was budgeted for rent and living expenses. There was no margin for error! Even a *hundred* less would mean I'd have to shuffle bills around. Two *thousand* less would mean I'd be coming home to a cold or dark (or both) apartment.

Back then, I wasn't as well-known a comedian. I wasn't what the clubs call a "name," which is why I believe ticket sales were initially slow. I'm guessing the club owner must've seen the early ticket numbers and decided he could make up for the short sales by paying me less (not the amount agreed upon in our contract). I was shocked and angry at what was happening, but I *needed* the money. So I told the booking agent to let the club owner know I'd be there as promised. But I was beside myself! I wanted this man to die! I wanted him to suffer! How dare he take money away from me! I couldn't let my contempt for this human being show.

NEVER SHOW YOUR ENEMY YOUR FACE

The next day, I flew in for the gig and there was no one from the club at the airport to pick me up. RED FLAG! With no choice, I took the $50 cab ride from JFK airport to my hotel in Mystic, Connecticut (the comedy club was housed inside the hotel). I checked in, showered, changed my clothes and prepared for my show, all before heading down to the club. I was still so upset and angry when I finally walked into the club that my hands were shaking all over the place. I was thinking nervously to myself the whole time, *You can do this! You have a plan! Just calm down! You don't want to blow this!*

When I saw Billy (the owner of the club), he was busy taking money and carefully watching over his cronies as they showed people to their seats. Without introducing myself, I did a quick scan of the room and noticed it looked pretty crowded. With that in mind, I walked over to the reservationist and casually asked, "How's tomorrow night looking?"

She replied, "Sold out."

I couldn't have been standing in front of the reservationist for more than a minute when Billy approached me from behind. Immediately, I could see by the guilty look on his face, he was uncomfortable about the whole money thing (after all, the room is packed!). As a matter of fact, he couldn't even look me in the eye! When we finally shook hands, he mealy-mouthed how sorry he was about the "confusion" with the money, but never said anything about paying my full contracted amount or not having someone meet me at the airport or even offering to reimburse me for the cab fare (excuse me, but did I just get off the boat?). I just smiled right back the whole time and then finally asked, "What the hell happened anyway?" See, it's not just *what* you say, it's *how* you say it. I was already rising above his game. Actually, I'd already formulated my own. I pretended to listen carefully as Billy double-talked his response to my question, trying to deflect blame away from himself and onto the booking agent. I let him finish before sarcastically saying, "Thank God it wasn't because of ticket sales, because that would've made me feel bad."

As we both continued to volley bullshit back and forth to each other, I wanted him to think he was in control (a key part of my plan). Also, you never want one club owner to say to another owner, "That Bobby, he's tough to work with." Because in this business, you can quickly be labeled the "heavy" (a bad guy) and that reputation sticks with you. Other club owners will use it against you in the future, making booking gigs more difficult. (Come on, I was learning and growing.)

Instead of letting my negative thoughts about Billy consume me, I found a way to disengage and focus on my craft. I enjoy thinking big and not allowing small-mindedness to enter my world, but when it does, I mentally focus on the task at hand. I keep my eye on the donut, not the hole! I know that the material I need to work out has both a rhythm and timing to it – I enjoy seeing that in my mind's eye and focusing on it. I delivered two dynamite shows to packed houses on Friday night, although I did promise myself *this is the last time I'll ever work for such a thief!* Because you never let someone take food out of your mouth!

As I was leaving the club Friday night, I said goodnight to Billy, but not before I sincerely added, "I don't want to get in between you and my booking agent over this money thing. I'm just here to work and hopefully this will all get resolved at some point." Even as I said it, I knew from experience, *if things aren't resolved at the time they're supposed to be, they'll never get resolved.* Now that I think about it, that might be a quote from the old TV show *Burke's Law* or maybe it was *Law & Order.* Either way, it doesn't matter. The point is, *I* knew the time to resolve this business with Billy was now... even if he didn't!

HOOK, LINE AND SINKER

On Saturday morning, I got up, worked out, wrote a little and then called the airline to find out what flights were available back to Los Angeles *that night!* It turned out there was a 10:30 pm flight out of JFK, arriving at LAX at 1:30 in the morning. So I tell the girl, "I have a ticket for Sunday morning, but I have a family emergency and need to get on that 10:30 pm flight tonight." After putting me on hold for a few minutes, she finally came back and told me, "No problem, Mr. Collins. I've canceled your flight for tomorrow and have you booked on the 10:30 pm departure tonight. Is there anything else I can do for you?"

On a side note, if you tried to change a flight's departure date and time today, you better have a no-limit credit card! Or at least be willing to donate a non-vital organ to anyone on the plane, should the need arise! Oh, how the planet has changed!

Knowing that both the 8 o'clock and 10 o'clock shows on Saturday night are sold out, I figured it was time to put my "Hook, Line and Sinker" plan into motion. I arrived at the showroom about twenty-five minutes early and stashed my packed bag by the side entrance near the service door behind a bush. Then I went back into the club and stood off to the side watching Billy once again do his "alpha-male" dog thing with his employees. After a few minutes, I went to the payphone that was within earshot of Billy and pretended to make a call to my booking agent. I started the pretend call by saying, "Hey, I don't want to be caught in the middle here. This is something you two need to work out." I can see out of the corner of my eye Billy has heard my end of the conversation, so I continue, "No, I'm not going to ask him that! Just leave me out of it!"

HOOKED!

As soon as I hung up the phone, Billy (who was now standing right beside me) said, "What was THAT all about?"

"My agent wants me to get paid in full, cash in hand, before I do tonight's shows."

"What?"

"I agree. I told him I thought it was a stupid idea. After all, I'm already at the club. What difference does it make if I get paid before or after I perform? While I know he wants to make sure I get my money, I think it's just an ego thing with him, you know? Look, you settle it with him; I'm going to check out the showroom. Let me know what you guys work out."

By now, Billy was all puffed up and ready to take on the world. He looked me right in the eye as he said with vengeance, "I'm not going to let anyone tell *me* how to run *my* club or pay *my* people. That's blackmail. You just let ME talk to him!"

With that, he stormed off toward his office to call my agent. But as anyone in this business *should* know, no one takes calls on Saturday night!

As I walked in the direction of the showroom, I had a smile on my face running from ear-to-ear and a bounce in my step. *I've got him on the LINE!*

A few minutes later, Billy came back to where I was standing a little red-faced, but I couldn't tell if it was from embarrassment or anger, since he wasn't able to reach my agent.

96

Another side note: just like a comic doesn't want to be saddled with the reputation of being difficult; club owners, while they may argue with booking agents, don't want to risk a booking agent passing (or telling other booking agents to pass) over their club. Club owners need booking agents to secure comics for their clubs, which gets butts in the seats and puts money in their pockets.

I guess Billy decided not to risk damaging the relationship with my booking agent (remember, he doesn't know the call was phony) and handed me a stack of cash for my services – mind you, the short, non-contractual stack!

Laughing as I took the money, I said, "Both you guys need to get on the same page. Because really, with two sold-out shows and one starting in ten minutes, where am I going?"

SINKER!

Keeping myself in Billy's direct line of vision, I stood with my cash in hand as I watched the room fill up. While the opening act was being introduced, I slowly sauntered over toward the men's room and then did a lickity-split around the corner and headed straight for the side entrance where my bag was stashed. Walking right out the service door, I hopped into a waiting cab with my bag over my shoulder, money in hand and NO regrets! Here I was, *Clyde Darrow Collins*, calculating as I'm riding toward the airport... the drive is about fifty minutes, the opening act will do his half hour and then the emcee will do his ten minutes, so I should be able to make a clean getaway!

Now, one should never underestimate the possible repercussions of taking action in such a drastic and public way, because once the other guy gets it into his head that he's right, there's always hell to pay! But you know what? By my code of honor, my grab-'n'-go was completely justified!

I took exactly the right amount of compensation – $2,500.00 – which was the original contracted amount. Sure, I left behind money for two Saturday night shows, but because he'd verbally broken the contract by changing the amount he would pay me from $5,000.00 to only $3,000.00, what I actually gave up amounted to about what he was going to short me. So in the end, I got paid just what I had contracted for – $1,250.00 per show! If you're going to play the game, you *have* to master it!

This story has since become folklore in the annals of comedy club history and, of course, I've heard many different versions of it over the years. Every time someone brings it up, I laugh and tell them the same thing, "You're a person first. What you do is not who you are. Just because you're a comic, doesn't mean you should ever let someone steal from you."

Shortly after my cash-'n'-dash with Billy, I heard from another comic he'd fallen on hard times. He lost his club, his home and the custody of his kids in a divorce and was now managing a theme restaurant.

Twelve years later, I was in New York again with my family for Thanksgiving. The day before the holiday, I took my kids to the theater for some fun. But before we went to the show, we stopped in this theme restaurant – *The Jekyll & Hyde Club* – for lunch. It's a scary place filled with mummies and grotesque, deathly-looking faces hanging on the walls. The staff even dressed up as characters from old horror movies. Once we were seated, the manager came over to our table and guess who it was? BINGO! Billy from Mystic, Connecticut! Looking down at our table, he asked, "Do you remember me?" Without hesitation, I replied, "*Absolutely*, I do."

He then told me through gritted teeth, "Do you realize you're the only person who's ever beat me out of money in my life?"

"I find that hard to believe... because it's *not* true. YOU beat YOURSELF out of that money when you failed to honor our contract."

Later, as we were leaving the restaurant, he followed my family and me to the door with another employee in tow (some guys just like cronies). Seeing this, I thought to myself, *nice to see you're still an asshole.* Standing in the doorway, he said to me as sarcastically as possible, "Hey, good luck in your career!"

"No," I responded, as I looked around, "Good luck in *yours!*"

Without even knowing it, Billy secured his loss at much more than just the game; he showed me his face – a face that reflected his sobering failure! Again, just the fact that I run into people who, for whatever reason, have a need to lie, cheat and steal from me and don't stop to think of the consequences their actions may have in their own lives, always amazes me.

But because I learned at an early age to never allow mean, petty people to stop or block or hinder me in any way, I've been able to achieve and maintain my goal: delivering my humor to audiences across the country without the attempted turmoil from *THOSE* kind of people!

Chapter 8
BEAUTY IS SKIN DEEP, BUT UGLY IS TO THE BONE

A while back, there was a reality TV show called *Extreme Makeover*. They took someone who basically resembled the Elephant Man – oh, come on – we've all seen someone on that show and thought, *Was there a pork chop hanging around your neck that made the dogs chew up your head?* OK, sorry, back to my point: the show would take a "Fido" and perform extensive plastic surgery while also giving them a new hairdo and a completely brand new wardrobe. They would then return these "made-over" people back to the herd. But the problem is you can't just tag these people and send them back to the pack. You know why? Because the pack won't accept them! It's the same as that old saying, "You can take the boy out of the country, but you can't take the country out of the boy." So, even though these people may now *look* beautiful, they're still drinking out of the same trough. Underneath their mask, they remain ugly. And ugly + ugly = *still ugly!*

This is just one example that gives me pause. Whatever happened to, "It's not what's on the outside that's important, it's what's on the inside that counts?" I know a lot of people who've changed their outsides because they thought that would change who they are, but don't they know? The outside projects what's on the inside, not the other way around! If you don't change the inside first, you're just putting the cart before the horse! True beauty really does come from the inside out. The outside in? Please!

Since strength comes with true beauty, and *true* beauty comes from the inside (which only God can supply) here's the simple fact: without God in your life, it doesn't matter what you do to your exterior, you'll never be more than a pretty structure built on top of a weak and ugly foundation. You can slap on as many coats of paint as you can afford (or put yourself in debt), but sooner or later, things will start to flake or peel and your ugly foundation *will* start to show. And God don't like ugly! Got it! Read on...

This is not to say that a woman who IS beautiful on the inside but unfortunately gets dealt a Wicked Witch of the West nose (or a gentle, sweet man that was unfortunately dealt a Jimmy Durante nose) should never make an improvement. Hey, even God misdeals once in a while – just look at the aardvark! So if a new honker is all it's going to take for someone to let their light shine through, I say do it. Just make sure you're changing your outside to *match* the inside, and not just trying to cover up a weak foundation!

You can *feel* when you're in the presence of a beautiful person, regardless (or even in spite of) their physical appearance. You know, it's that someone you meet and see a glow, a light to them. You can't put your finger on it, but there's an enticing aura about them – they pull you toward them. This person makes you feel good about yourself and everything else. You can relax and let your guard down. There's an energy swirling around them that feels so positive and right. Their splendor radiates so strongly from the inside that the package housing their luminosity is virtually invisible. This person proffers no judgments or falsehoods; they are *genuinely* beautiful. You just know there's something special about them – they know and you know that their moral compass is complete. Their spiritual path has taken shape. Simply being who they are will make you want to be a better person. They can see your whole story and somehow make looking at yourself a lighter and easier experience. You know what I'm talking about? You'll hear people say about such a person "everything she touches turns to gold." It's not material wealth they're referring to, it's their essence enriching your soul!

On the other hand, there's the UGLY; the person who can see the insecurity of another and chooses to use it for their own means to control, manipulate, take from and put down, rather than inspire, teach, and show a better way. They are the examples of what we should not be. It's almost like God provides us these people to learn from; to not be intimidated by; to not allow them to enter our aura. He's showing us this is not what life's about – the shallowness, the fear, the conning, the deceitful way these people operate. Because of their *own* insecurities and hurt, they've chosen to focus on other peoples' weak points – and that's UGLY!

I run across these ugly people all the time, and I always make it a point to leave them with a compliment or a good word. Something that hopefully inspires them to spread the good and lift up someone else. "Pay it forward" is a choice. Look, we're not all in a position to reach the masses, but one-on-one is a great start and trust me, it works!

We've all known people who, when they walk into a room, the lights dim – it's what they carry with them. They're negative, sad, judgmental, and looking to latch on to someone they can pull down into their own psychological shit pile. We won't give them a voice here. Just remember that they exist, and you should always try to avoid them if and when you can!

I know this lady – she's forty-something, with a lot going on. She is college-educated, responsible, kind, tall and athletic. But even with all these positives, she can't seem to find anyone to spend her life with.

First, I think it's important to share that this woman has had some cosmetic surgery. Actually, she's had *a lot* of cosmetic surgery, surprisingly in more places than I could ever imagine! Somewhere along her journey, it seems she lost her self-confidence and started to believe the ribbon on the outside is more important than the gift on the inside. If I had to guess, I'd say it happened after the thousandth time her family insinuated... *Well, there must something wrong with you. You're the oldest, the only daughter and the only one who's not married!*

Remember a while back when I told you about my sixth sense? Well, it's not just confined to reading an audience. I can look into the eyes of someone I know and see *everything* about them, even things they thought they'd convincingly covered over.

I know, it's pretty cool, huh?

When I look into this woman's eyes, I see a lonely, sad

102

girl who's ashamed she's allowed herself to become *one of those women* (and men) who constantly changes his/her outside in order to feel worthy. A woman who deep down is a frightened girl who has let her parents' (and even her friends') ugly and damaging remarks seep into her psyche and poison her self-confidence. A person who's convinced herself that the very high standards she's set for herself and the men she occasionally dates, are necessary in order for her to find THE perfect mate. But in reality, these standards (perhaps unwittingly) have served only to act as a self-fulfilling prophecy. She's never found out what *she really* wants – which is a nice, regular guy who she can marry and raise a family with.

The problem (as I see it) is actually quite simple. She needs to stop tightening her chin, reshaping her nose and pulling up her eyes, thinking each cosmetic surgery will finally make her into this *new* person, a better person... because it WON'T!

She is a prime example (but certainly not the only one) of someone who should stop looking into a mirror for affirmation. She needs to accept and acknowledge the true being she has *always been* – a loving, beautiful woman, who is her own person, so that every time she hears that inner voice telling her she's not good enough, she can counter with confidence, "I am *more than good enough.* I will go out with someone because they make me feel good about myself and not because of my looks or material possessions. I will look for the good in other people. I will enjoy my time on this planet. If (when) I discover I need a Q & A, along this newly chosen path, I will first ask God, then my *real* friends, to help me along the way."

Once she re-examines, re-evaluates and revamps her inside self, her self-esteem will be re-established and it will become easier each day for her to *see* the change she wants to be!

Well, there you go. I just saved her a lot of time and money on a shrink. *They call 'em shrinks for a reason.* I know a psychiatrist or two and just look at them!

103

I think it was Albert Einstein who said, "Insanity is doing the same thing over and over again, but expecting different results." For this lady, and all the other Mr. & Ms. Potato Heads out there, enough is enough. None of you are fooling anyone! People who've had work done just look like they've had work done! Kenny Rogers of all people should've known it was time to fold 'em! And Dolly Parton – I'm surprised those hot stage lights haven't melted her into a sparkly, spangled puddle by now! Then there's Melanie Griffith. Honey, Antonio Banderas was a handsome man when you married him. He's still a handsome man. Don't you think it freaks him out a little to see your surprised face all the time?

Until *you* believe in yourself, and also understand your outside isn't what makes you worthy, you'll only continue to cover up the problem. What makes a person worthy is a good, kind and beautiful spirit. Nourish, value and present this to the world and good things will happen. Reach out to people; give a compliment and take some time to see yourself, and when you see those same insecurities in another person, use that as a reminder to continue to work on yourself! It's all going to be OK.

I next want to address those people who simply didn't win at genetic roulette... and you have to admit, there are quite few of those folks out there! But, at the same time, a lot of them also possess an *inner* beauty that is so strong and positive, it completely negates their exterior. These are the people who emanate a beautiful spirit. I *like* people like this. They add to life, not take away from it.

I had a friend, Christina, who has since passed. When she was alive, there were plenty of people who thought of her as unattractive, even ugly, because of her size. She weighed about 450 pounds, but I always thought of her as a beautiful person, in *every* sense of the word. Speaking with her was always a gift, and laughing with her (which was most of the time) was a trip! She had such wisdom about life – she was smart, well read and fun to be around! The only time her physical size ever registered with me was when we'd be out in public. Then I'd notice people staring at her with judgment in their eyes. When this happened, I wanted to scream at them, "If you people only had a finger nail of what this lady has inside her, your life would be a whole lot better!" But it's sad to say, I knew it wouldn't do any good.

I think we all know people who have naturally pretty exteriors wrapped around a very ugly core. I have met many people like this in my lifetime – people whose ugly runs so deep, it's drowned out anything good that ever existed, and they are now walking, talking and breathing evil. I don't mean someone who exhibits an occasional random act of ugliness (we all stumble once in a while); I'm talking about people who are *pure* evil... evil for evil's sake! While I don't want to give these people too much of a presence here, I do intend to show you why I believe what I do, which is that true inner beauty always triumphs over ugly, *even* hardcore evil. Because anytime I've ever witnessed beauty look ugly or evil in the eye – ugly or evil always blinks!

As you have seen by now, Jill believes in the adage, "True giving is giving with no expectation of receiving." One way she practices this is by sitting on the board of a special needs camp that Madison now attends every summer in Lincoln, Vermont, called Zeno Mountain Farm. In addition to being on the board, every year we hold an outdoor fundraising party for the camp in front of our house. We invite all the neighbors, and also ask our neighbors to sign off on the party. This way, we can obtain the necessary permits, including one to close off the street for the night. We set everything up right in front of our house in the street – tables, chairs, food, live music, *you name it*. This is no little cook out!

After many years of organizing and hosting this fundraiser, it's become somewhat of a neighborhood tradition. Everyone (well, *almost* everyone) looks forward to it. It's what I believe "community" to be at its finest. For me, the personal reward is seeing the looks on people's faces and watching their hearts open up as they interact with the campers. A large number of them attend the party with their family and friends, everyone showing support for the cause – and the campers always put on a "show," a staged performance that allows everyone to see the real people who exist beneath those damaged exteriors.

While the party requires a huge amount of planning and work, the benefits are *immense*. The joy it brings everyone serves as an example of why it's so important to support Zeno Mountain Farm (and other services for the disabled). They truly are wonderful! But the real accomplishment of the party is to remind everyone that *we're all not that different from each other*; a reminder that hopefully each attendee carries with them the next time they encounter a disabled person.

Every year, our permits expire at 11:00 pm, and every year this old couple that lives only a few houses away calls the police to complain about the noise and the blocked street. When the police show up (it's policy for them to respond to all noise complaints), I simply wave our permits at them like a geisha in drag, doing the fan-dance of seduction. This never fails to get them laughing, and every year they simply shake their heads and then GPS right over to the food table. Or they seek out someone (usually a kid), to see how they're doing. Even a first-time "rookie" never just turns around and leaves right away. It seems a little mingling with civilians does both persuasions a world of good!

But what happened this past year? Jill handed me a bouquet of flowers and said, "Bobby, I want you to go over to Mr. and Mrs. Crotchitypants' house and personally invite them to the party. Make it sound like YOU really want them here. Tell them how much fun you think it will be for them. Also, let them know there'll be free food and a live band, and they can come dance. Make them think they'll just have an overall *wonderful* time."

Now you know another reason why I married this woman! Her heart is bigger than mine... and that's what I need in my life!

Since I've honestly had enough of these people over the years, I responded, "You want me to 'make nice' to old Crotchitypants and that shriveled up crone he's married to? Nope, sorry, you got the wrong huckleberry for your little job. No way. I want to see those ugly, disgusting, vile, heartless, insensitive, poor excuses for human beings reduced to piles of dust until the winds carry them off the face of the earth!"

"Bobbbbyyyyyy," Jill said in her syrupy "Don't be an asshole" tone. "For all we know, they may have serious health problems, or lost a child, or maybe they're... well, you know, old and just plain scared."

Reluctantly, I walked off in the direction of their house,

David Arquette, Lou Ferrigno, and Bobby. "You have the right to remain... HUGE!"

muttering, "Just plain scary, if you ask me," (once Jill is out of earshot!)

When I got to the Crotchitypants' house, I knocked on their door with a fist full of flowers and a smile plastered across my face. While I'm waiting for someone to open the door, I can hear footsteps approaching, but the door doesn't open. Instead, I see Mr. Crotchitypants standing at the front window, "What do you want?" he bellowed.

Oh, OK, I see, so now I'm the Big Bad Wolf? Well, bring it on! I'm going to just huff and puff and... but before I said anything, I could hear Jill inside my head again, *Bobbbbyyyyyy, maybe they're just old and scared.* So, I took a breath and just short of being the Music Man, I projected my image into the window. "When was the last time you took your bride to a dance with great food, fun people and good music, without even having to leave your block? Well, sir, I'm here to tell you today's your lucky day! Because I'd like to invite both of you to our party tonight! And *look* (I hoist my bouquet with community theater gusto), I've even brought some lovely flowers!"

"Get off my porch!" he yelled back. "Keep your flowers, and I *will* be calling the police tonight!"

"Why are you like this?" New York Bobby snapped back. "These are special people who need our help!"

"Get off my porch! I'm not going to tell you again!" And with that, he disappeared out of sight.

Walking back home, I admit, I ran several horrible death scenarios through my head, each more grizzly and gruesome than the last. But by the time I reached our yard, I simply said to myself, *some people...* and let it go.

That night (just as expected), they called the police. And as usual, the police showed up, checked our paperwork and then joined the festivities.

Now here's the kicker to this whole thing. Since then, an English family has moved in right next door to Mr. and Mrs. Crochitypants, complete with three extremely loud, jumping off the roof, tearing in and out of the driveway, blasting loud music, totally wild-child teenagers! The old couple has already called the police on the family five times and they've lived there less than a year! Ah, there is some justice in the world.

But I have to admit, at Halloween, I still fantasize about egging their house and pulling down their front porch! However, since the British invasion, I'm sure they've installed security cameras, and that kind of evidence would be tough to deny!

In the end, Mr. and Mrs. Crochitypants serve as an example of sorts for the neighborhood. They are a reminder to everyone to never allow ugly to take a foothold and grow in your heart!

Much earlier in my career, I got a call two weeks before Christmas to work at a hotel casino in Atlantic City. I was excited because this was a place I'd wanted to work for a long time, but didn't feel I was quite ready for it yet.

"Bobby, we'll pay you $5,000 for seven shows," the club owner told me. At the time, this was a virtual fortune! He went on to say, "The shows run from Tuesday night through Sunday night, which includes both Christmas Eve and Christmas Day." When I heard this last part, two thoughts immediately ran through my head: *One, whoever said, "The show must go on" is an asshole! (Unless, of course, it's me – in that case, there's always an exception!) and Two, I hope I haven't sold myself short on the fee.*

After thinking everything through, I finally told the club owner, "In my world, Christmas Day is completely reserved for my family. I can come in for the rest of the shows, but I'm gonna have to skip Christmas..."

Before I could even get the word "Day" out of my mouth, he freaked out on me, "Take it or leave it!"

With lightning fast rationalizations shooting through my head, *You've been wanting to break into this club for a long time... You can really use the five thousand bucks... Christmas is just another day...* I reactively answered, "I'll take it!"

As soon as I hung up the phone on that cold winter day, I remembered Jill (who wasn't yet my wife), saying to me,

"What was that call about? Your whole demeanor changed while you were talking."

Without thinking, I responded in anger, "What do you mean my whole demeanor changed? What are you? The conversation police?" Even as I said those words, I knew deep down, I was using her innocent question as a reason to initiate an argument and wrongly deflect my anger and disappointment with myself onto her.

Before she could justifiably come back at me *(oh, another reason our relationship works so well... Jill has never backed away from getting in my shit when I'm being an asshole)*, I caught myself and confessed the real problem, "Jill, I can't work Christmas Day. I might be throwing away the opportunity I've been waiting for, and maybe I'll never be asked to work there again, but I *fucked* up. I can't take this gig. I should have told him, 'No.' Besides, who wants to work for some prick who keeps his club open on Christmas day? What kind of Scrooge fails to understand the importance of family? And I don't mean just for me, but for all his club employees!"

A few minutes later, I called the club owner back and told him, "I'm sorry, but like I said, Christmas is a special time of year, and I always spend it with my family. If a date opens up in the future, I would love the opportunity to work your club. Thank you again for the offer." I was hoping he would say something like, "OK, how about we book you for a date in, let's say, February?"

Instead, I got an angry, "I don't think there'll be another time for you!"

CLICK!

OK, wait a minute. Am I the only one picking up a pattern here? Apparently there are large segments of businessmen out there seriously lacking any type of telephone etiquette. I guess they don't teach that at Asshole Business Academy. Sorry to interrupt, but that was really bothering me.

As soon as I heard the line go dead, my heart sank. Right away, I slipped back into that old routine and started blaming myself. *I must've done something wrong. I'm not a good person.* At the same time, my head started spitting out:

110

Did I do the wrong thing? What is the right thing? Who is the bad guy here? Then for a split second, my career jumped to the head of line, *What if this guy calls every club in the country and has me blackballed!* Thankfully, just as quickly, my priorities realigned themselves. *No! Family and Christmas Day are not for sale!* As soon as this last thought crystallized, my heart was comforted, knowing I'd made the right decision.

Might is indeed right (and pays better, too!). Because two days after Christmas, someone from *Mr. I don't think there'll be another time for you* Casino Hotel called me and said, "The comic that was booked to open up for Dionne Warwick is sick. We need a last-minute replacement. Please understand, this is for one night only, but the pay is $7,500. Do you want the gig?"

Now with justified resolve, I responded, "Of course! Just tell me what time and where to go!"

When I arrived at the appointed day and time, I waited downstairs (as instructed) at the hotel casino's comedy club room, which seats 250 people. Next thing I know, I'm ushered upstairs to the much larger 1,200-seat theater. Hey, they weren't going to get any complaints from me!

After my show was over, I stopped back down at the comedy club room to peek in. And guess what? The Scrooge who wanted me to work Christmas came over to me like we're two long-lost pals. Suddenly, he's the nicest guy in the world, "Hey, Bobby, I heard you had a great show up there tonight. You know, that earlier thing, that was... um... uh," then with a big shit-eating grin, he said, "Well, you know... that was just business." The whole time he was talking, I just kept thinking, *Yeah, smile all you want! I know your ugly heart! You keep telling yourself, it's "just business!"* I knew in my heart this man placed the almighty dollar ahead of the Almighty and his family. Finally, he ended our conversation with, "I've got some dates I want to run by you. This way we can get you booked back in here. You have some time to do that?"

So, did I work for him? You bet I did! I'm not the guy who cuts off his nose to spite his face. I'm a comic. It's how I put food on the table. My office is all over the country, in comedy clubs, casinos, theaters, even the boom-boom room at the Holiday Inn. I don't have to like all the owners I work for (I'm sure some of you dislike your boss), or even respect them for that matter (although, there are many who I both like and respect). It's the fact that he knew that *I knew* just how ugly he really was that allowed me to work his club, confident in the knowledge that I'll always be treated as nothing less than a consummate professional. But you know what? To this day, he still can't really look me in the eyes. Me? I stare right into his and smile!

Here's the thing – once ugly rears its ugly head, it eventually turns its negativity on its host. I've since heard this man has lost two of the three comedy clubs he owns, has become an alcoholic and even filed a lawsuit against his own daughter! It always rears its ugly face!

Readers, the lesson here is this: when you follow your heart and do the right thing, you'll always be able to look the other person right in the eyes with no regret or shame. Remember, beauty always trumps ugly! Once you accept and follow this universal principle, you'll find that if a door gets slammed in your face, God will always open a back window!

I'm a firm believer that if you live an ugly life, ugly will catch up with you as you age. While the cumulative effects may go unnoticed as they're happening, eventually years and years of ugly will manifest itself in its most obvious form, the *physical.* I've seen people literally get devoured from the inside out with various diseases – cancer, diabetes, and tumors – because they lived an ugly life. Never doubt for a minute that an ugly heart doesn't have the power to deform the human body!

I'm not saying that every time anyone is afflicted by a debilitating illness it's because they *are* ugly. But, and this is a big BUT, just one time, I would love to hear someone say, "If Mary had only lived a fruitful life, helped others, grew in spirit and applied herself to being a better person instead of sucking the life out of everything she touched, maybe she wouldn't be in the position she's in right now." Instead, people lament, "It's *so awful* about Mary's cancer, the way she's *suffering* right now." While I know this will never happen, I use it as an example to illustrate that you should never discount how you live your life and treat others, thinking it doesn't matter. Because, it *does* matter! Ugly will catch up with you. If you live ugly, you die ugly! Not hard to understand, is it?

One summer, I was cashing in my reward for working a lot of cruise ship shows, using my earned free time to enjoy the beaches and the sun. I was sporting a George Hamilton-caliber tan and working that smile, too! Which may have had something to do with a friend of mine asking me to go to a luncheon that was just for her family and friends (this was before I met Jill). I knew she really wanted me to go, and I was also pretty sure she had talked me up to her friends!

When I arrived at the luncheon, my friend greets me and I could see right away she was all excited to introduce me to everyone. She first pointed out her mother on the other side of the room and said, "Come on, I want to introduce you two." I realized as we started making our way across the room, her mother was the woman who practically did a Linda Blair-style head turn when I first walked in. As we were standing in front of her mother (before I can even say hello), she loudly blurted out, "Are you a black man? A Negro?" Most of the people in the room were simultaneously surprised, stunned and openly embarrassed! Especially, since anyone could plainly see I was neither! *But then, so what if I was?*

To say the least, my poor friend was horrified by not only the words her mother had just vomited, but the ugly propellant used to deliver them. Again, it was up to me to muster up beauty to stare down ugly! To set the example and overcome the smallness! To kill her mother with kindness (and humor) for the benefit of everyone in the room, but most importantly for her mother!

Without so much as a blink of an eye, I confidently replied, "Yes, ma'am, in fact, I am. I can dance better than most people, I'm more athletic *and* because I'm a black man, I learned early on to overcome prejudice. This way, at times like this, I don't let that ugly serpent inside me strike out to embarrass myself or the people I love." Then I just stood there

113

smiling at her, breaking the tension in the room. I successfully won the crowd over with humor and for the rest of the luncheon, I was the undisputed life of the party!

As I was getting ready to leave, I went over to my friend's mother and told her, "I'd like to thank you for having such a wonderful daughter." Then I politely took her hand and added, "It was so nice to have met you." And that was it. Beauty-1, Ugly-0! But you have to know, even the victor gets banged up on the field of battle. And I won't lie, this one made a mark!

All the people I've talked about so far in this chapter (and believe me, there are plenty of others I left out!), have not aged gracefully. Ugly has left its mark in different ways on each and every one of them. Bottom line – there are a lot of sad, unhappy, damaged people in this world (with different degrees of ugly in their heart), hiding their shame or pain behind some type of mask.

But maybe that's why I'm a comic – a clown! I see humor as the purest form of truth. I use it as tool to pry off everyone's mask... well, at least long enough for them to face the ugliness and stare it down! If only one person leaves my show each night determined to make a change because they recognized they *are* the ugly person I revealed through a joke or story I shared from the stage, then I'm a happy person. To this day, I remain grateful for the path I've chosen, while also rejoicing in the fact that I'm able to witness beauty stare down ugly. I can't emphasize this message *enough*... God don't like ugly!

Of all the chapters, lessons, anecdotes, confessions, examples and words I've put down on these pages, this subject matter was by far my least favorite. Not because I had to struggle to find what it was I wanted to share, but because it was the closest to my heart. I needed to choose carefully which stories I wanted to write about, and whether any of what I was about to repeat might possibly be hurtful to those I hold dear in my life. These decisions necessitated more than one little chat with God; that much I can tell you! In the end, I don't feel any of what I've shared is hurtful. However, should anyone take

114

offense with what I've written, I wholeheartedly apologize, as this was never my intent.

Chapter 9
SHAKE, RATTLE AND ROLL

I'd first like to say, there aren't too many things in life that actually get me rattled. I guess, we all like to think of ourselves as Superman, or at the very least Clark Kent – invincible to most outside threats. But what a crock!

I came home not too long ago after being on the road for a week and with my bags in hand, Hallie rushed up to me and shouts "Daddy! You really need to talk to your *wife*! I'm telling you, that woman is *crazy!*" Does this SHAKE me up? Absolutely not. *This* I can handle. I just bobbled my head like a Lakers give-away doll and then went to find Jill, and continued to bobble in agreement with *her* side of the story. After she finished, I went back to Halle and translated the Queen's proclamation (using interpretative skills I've very carefully developed over the years) while reminding her of the matriarchal hierarchy of the Collins Castle. I finished by telling her that while the position of Princess (and even King) does provide certain perks, it does NOT yield any real power. All the while I was trying not to let her see my backbone slipping out of my ass!

Folks, all we can hope for in our daily lives, whether it's family, house problems, money, job security, co-workers, travel, *whatever*... is harmony. When day-to-day life is humming along smoothly, it's a beautiful thing. But when it's not, you have to handle it quickly and try not to let anyone go to bed angry. Which is why when things (and people) around me get out of tune, or I witness (or am made a part of) an act of personal injustice (someone just not playing fair or operating with an air of entitlement – you know, that cutting-in-line type of injustice!) – *that* is what SHAKES my tree!

I was in my office one day in the summer of 2005 when I got a phone call.

"Is this Bobby Collins, the comedian?"

"Yes, it is. How may I help you?"

"I'm the producer of the *Judge Judy Show*. We'd like to know if you would consider coming on our show here in Los Angeles."

I like Judge Judy. She calls it straight when dealing with all those sleazebags and puss pods of society. But before I answered, I thought, *Why me? Do they feel Judge Judy is too hard for TV and want to lighten things up with a comic? Have someone in the courtroom that can pull off playing serious, yet provide some humorous fodder?*

The producer then told me, "Since you're being sued anyway, we thought you might want to kick it over to us. To have it 'heard' on TV. We pay whether you win or lose. So, really, it's a win-win situation."

My ass closed up tighter than one of those right-wing Tea Party conservative nut jobs! WHAT? I'm being sued? Who would sue me? I'm the defender of the truth! A win-win? Bullshit! I'm not going to place my reputation on the line to go on the *Judge Judy* show. By the way, have you ever seen men on that show? Most of them leave carrying their balls in their hands, crying and finding God at the water fountain. If you take the percentage of cases involving men vs. women and compare who is adjudicated victorious – no man in his right mind would *ever* go on that show! Besides, what type of person goes on a show like that to hang their dirty laundry out for everyone to see? A *moron*, that's who!

Finally, I said, "Apparently you know more than I do. Who, exactly, is suing me?"

The producer shared the name of a woman (past acquaintance), who out of the blue had chosen to seriously RATTLE my world!

I won't mention this woman's name. Why? Because she's still living, and although I seriously doubt she has many friends, I don't want the few she may have to come crawling out from under her same rock! Besides, I don't think it's a nice thing to do. We all have parents or a partner or kids who love us, so who am I to remove her mask and reveal the gargoyle? Plus, that thing called karma keeps popping into my head. Am I naïve or just a sentimentalist at heart? Who knows? But I've also been indoctrinated by TV and newspaper stories over the years that tell you (even if you're innocent) you can spend tons of money and time just fighting to tell the truth. So, even though you might win in the end, you lose a hell of a lot along the way proving it!

A little background on this woman who filed the lawsuit: years ago, a friend of mine owned a comedy club, the *East Side Comedy Club* on Long Island. This particular woman worked in the office at the club and back in those days, comics and club workers were a close-knit group. If you worked in a club, in any capacity, you were aware that all comics are traveling circus people, or carnie folk, as I like to refer to my breed. We go into a venue, do the required amount of shows, act professionally, don't rock the boat, get paid and move on. That's the drill.

So twenty years later, the night before Thanksgiving, 2004, I was out on Long Island doing a couple of shows at a club called *Governor's* (an annual Thanksgiving date). In between my shows, I went to the bar to get a drink and there's a woman sitting there with a big smile on her face. It took a second for me to place her, but then I realized I know her from the now defunct *East Side Comedy Club*. I gave her a big hug hello and before I knew it, she asked me for a favor. "Bobby, would you be willing to headline a benefit show for cystic fibrosis on Long Island at the Westbury Music Theater?" She then went on to tell me the date and names of the other performers who'd be there, too (some are past cohorts of mine). She ended her pitch with, "You'll have a lot of fun and you'll also be helping out a good cause."

I responded by explaining, "Because I have a daughter born with a chromosome disorder, I do a certain number of benefit shows for charities related to special needs children. But, to be honest, the date of October 22nd (the following year) is a tough one for me to commit to." I said this because for me and every other comic, October is open season (*read* big money time!). The summer is over, the kids are back in school and that's the time when we usually secure our really good paying gigs – corporate events, private parties, theater appearances, Las Vegas shows or just really good comedy club dates. The "money season" runs from October through the first half of December and then picks up again from February through May. Those are our bankable months and we need those!

I finished up by telling her, "I'm sorry, but I can't do the event." Not one to take no for an answer, she countered with a money offer, which was only about a third of the amount I usually get for a paid gig on that date. "It's not about the money," I told her. "It's the time of year. I'm sorry, but maybe I'll consider it again in the future." She kept pleading and I felt uncomfortable, so I sheepishly responded, "OK, I'll do it. However, just so you know, I'm saying yes with the condition that should a paying gig come in for that date, I'll have to cancel on you."

After I got back to my office in California, I received a contract in the mail and I signed it (knowing that I've told her I may have to cancel). It's worth mentioning here that in the land of comics, it really is a small world of carnie folk. We cut and paste gigs all the time to make things work. We cancel and move shows around with the utmost respect, *at least within the carnie tribes who value their integrity.* It all seems to work out in the end, with no one (clubs and comics) really losing.

When July of 2005 rolled around, my office assistant tells me, "This woman from Long Island keeps calling and wants to talk to you about the October 22nd event she has set up with you."

Since I wasn't sure what she was talking about, I asked her, "Can you go through my October calendar and see if I have a contract lined up for that date?"

When she found the file, she told me, "You have a signed contract on the 22nd to do a show for the alumni of an upstate New York College."

Once I heard this, it took a minute before I finally recalled the cystic fibrosis event on Long Island. I immediately picked up the phone and called this woman back, "I'm sorry," I told her, "but I'm going to have to cancel on you. However, if you want, I can find another comic to take my place so you'll have the same number of comics in the line-up. I also would

119

like to make a $1,000 donation to help the cause."

Initially she sounded disappointed when I broke the news, but then her demeanor instantly changed to snitty! So I calmly reminded her, "There's no way you should be surprised

The last weekend show to be performed at the famous Sands Hotel, Las Vegas Strip, before it was demolished.

by this. I explicitly told you when we discussed this event, the date was iffy for me to begin with. I have to support my family, which is why I told you if a paid gig presented itself, I would have to cancel on you."

After a moment of silence, she said, "Well, I think the least you could do is pay for the posters I printed up." *Unbelievable! Who prints posters for an event four months out?*

"No way," I told her. "I'm sorry. That was never part of any deal!"

At hearing my outrage, she started backpedalling, "Well, I haven't actually had the posters printed yet, but the layout is done. All that's left for me to do is take the file to the printer. I think you should compensate me for that much at least. But, if you would just come do the show, it would make everything so much easier."

Hoping for what will *finally* be the last time, I said, "I'm sorry. I can't do the event. Maybe next year." The conversation over, I hung up and, in my mind, that was that – finished – over and done.

Which is why, about a month later, I was totally surprised and caught off-guard when I got the call from the producer of the *Judge Judy* show! Suddenly I felt the tide rising all around me. For a few panicked moments, all I could do was tread water! Then I decided to call this woman back to again offer her a $1,000 donation (hoping to make all of this go away). But no, she's developed a hump with one hair and has become vindictive! She responded, "I don't want your $1,000! You need to pay me $5,000!"

Five thousand dollars? This cretin wanted me to hand over $5,000?! My confidence in the gene pool was once again waning. Not only was I RATTLED by her actions, I was kicking myself for signing the contract *she* sent (believing she would honor our conversation about the probability of cancellation) instead of using *my* own contract, which contains my standard cancellation clause. I wasn't sure a court of law would see beyond what is black and white and recognize the fact that I'm nothing more than a target of opportunity for this woman. Did I sign our contract? Yes. Did I break our contract? Yes. Did I do exactly what I told her I might do? Yes. Did this make me a bad guy? No. All it meant was I made a bad decision by caving in and agreeing to do the charity gig in the first place, then foolishly thinking she had the integrity to abide by our conversation! All I'd gotten for doing exactly what I told her I would do is get served with papers! Another hard lesson learned!

121

After gathering my emotions, I finally told her, "Absolutely not. I'm not giving you $5,000." Especially since I know she'd already replaced me with a fine comic named Sal Richards, so her "show" was still intact.

A few days later, I was playing basketball (*yes*, slow, middle-aged white guys play basketball) with my friend Robert Cheri, who happens to be an attorney (*yes*, some attorneys have friends). When we were done with our game, I ran the whole scenario by him. He told me with a laugh, "Hey Bobby, if this is the only amount you're ever sued for, you're way ahead of the game." *Easy for him to say!* He then went on to tell me, "I got this one, OK? Let me handle it."

I figured why not? He'd already done some "buddy" legal work for me in the past, so I told him, "Deal. I'll get all the paper work over to you."

On my court day, I put my suit on and went to meet Robert at the courthouse, only to be informed my case had been dropped "with prejudice." Ahh, I can breathe again! I never understood how someone could be such a lowlife, moneygrubber to begin with. But wait, what does this "with prejudice" thing mean? What does she think now? That I'm some sort of overseer? Another white man working to keep the black man down? It turns out that *NO*, that's not what it means. What it *does* mean in this case, is the next day I'm once again served with papers, only this time she's asking for $100,000! The pirates have fired across the bow and are attempting to clamber over the rails! The journey continued...

This whole Long Island thing made me ask, *What has happened to the principle of putting good out into the universe so good will come back to you?* Hey, I'm allowed to ask this question, especially now that I'm known as "The Defendant" on some court docket. Is it too much to ask for people to take responsibility; to be kind and help each other; to expect the best out of everyone? OK, maybe I am being a baby here, but damn it, *Why do I have to go through a bunch of shit (again)?*
I'd already learned *one* important lesson through this ordeal, which was, I don't want to experience this whole mess! Besides, don't you think God can see I'm a bit mature for a

growth spurt? I don't want to spend months, maybe years, waiting for a litigated resolution. I'm an American... I want to know now! I want things to happen when I want them to! I thought if I handled things the Right Way (as best as I could), everything would turn out for the best.

WRONG! You know why? Because it just doesn't happen that way! You never stop growing, and to grow, you gotta have the shit! God knows this! If you push a bean down into a big steamy pile of shit, you'll see a big old sturdy stalk break through and wind its way up to the clouds (What? You don't think Jack went through some shit?).

OK, back to the saga of Long Island. My attorney, Robert, informed me since I signed the event contract in California (Santa Monica), this is where the case should be heard. However, this woman's lawyer filed a motion to have the case moved to New York (where she lives) and also has filed another motion to have it heard before the New York Superior Court. He then got right to the bottom line, "Bobby, I think we're probably going to win the case, but in order to keep it in California, we're going to have to argue for it. And that means another $5,000 to $8,000. Plus, another $10,000 once we do go to court."

Taking all this in, I was thinking, *Fuck! If it costs that much to WIN, how much will it cost me if I LOSE!* But I dismissed this thought and reminded myself this *isn't* about the money (but I'll be honest, I hadn't expected it to be so much) – it's about *walking the talk*. After all, I've brought up my girls to always stand behind their convictions, to believe "Might is right," even when it's scary! I don't want them to think I've just been *talking the talk* this whole time. That getting doused with a bucket of $18,000 is all it takes to turn me into the Wicked Witch of the West... *Melting... melting... I'm melting!*

Then there's that whole reality of being tried by a jury of your peers. Norm Crosby said it best: when you go into court, you are putting your fate into the hands of twelve people who weren't smart enough to get out of jury duty.

ACCKKK!

After all this, I was left with two choices: (1) Either

123

work out an offer that will satisfy Cruella de Vil or (2) take my chances with the dimwitted dozen. I went with what was behind door number one! The attorneys worked out a deal. This sad, disgusting, mercenary agreed to settle for $3,000. I say *mercenary* because during the negotiations, I learned only a small portion of the money she raised ever got donated to cystic fibrosis, *the rest she keeps for herself!* (Robert told me this is a fairly common practice.) Even so, I couldn't help but wonder when Robert asked her attorney, "Do you think the New York Attorney General's office might find your client's source of income interesting?" if *that's* what helped her decide to settle out of court rather than pursue the original $100,000 action.

A few days later, while I was writing out the check in Robert's office for him to mail to her attorney, I learned something else. Settlements always go through the attorney, which guarantees they get their fee paid first. As I signed the check, I let out a sigh and told him how this whole process has left me disillusioned about our entire legal system. Grinning, he said, "Welcome to my world of scum!" As he's putting my check into his file he added, "By the way, just so you know, you got off cheap!"

You have to understand, I was brought up in New York. By the age of twelve I'd seen transvestites, rats with leather jackets, rats walking mice, *you name it.* I didn't think anything could SHAKE me. But I have to be honest, this situation did. The biggest lesson I learned through this fiasco is that the days of taking someone at their word are gone. You can't count on a handshake to be binding anymore. You have to have a contract, and in that contract every "T" has to be crossed and every "I" dotted *'cause ain't no one gonna look out for you 'cept you!*

So while you should never place money before God or family, you have to respect the dollar. Money in and of itself isn't bad; it's how people use it. Truth is, I wrote off the $3,000, and I never again used anyone else's contract other than my own, so I guess I just needed a reminder to let this kind of stuff more readily ROLL off my back. To better understand, this wasn't about *me* – this wasn't *personal* – these were the actions of someone who placed money above integrity. Someone who hadn't learned that if your heart is in the right place, your wallet will always be full.

A few months later, I received an email from this same woman. It read, and I quote, "Bobby, you probably don't want to ever speak to me again, but you mentioned you had a special needs child. Maybe this year we could do the charity for her?"

A line from the movie *Munich* instantly flashed through my head: *It just keeps going on and on and on... Won't they ever learn?*

I was stunned for a brief moment. I just sat there staring at the screen with ugly thoughts racing through my head like, *Die bitch! They'll never find your body!* My fingers were poised. I was ready to unleash what I hoped would be recognized someday as the most vile, wrathful, in-your-face, fuck-you-with-a-household-utensil, a thousand-year-pox-on-your-descendants email ever typed!

As my finger came down on the letter "D," my spiritual voice suddenly interrupted my train of thought. *Bobby, breathe. You need to clear out all this ugliness and think back to why this came about in the first place.* Taking my finger off the letter "D," I was able to reaffirm that way back before all the bullshit and legalese and wasted time and money, the simple truth was I'd extended an act of kindness to her by agreeing to perform at her charity event for a fee that was far below my normal rate.

Sitting tall, I now confidently wrote back, "In life, you might end up with a lot of money in the bank, but to me, you'll always be a soulless, sad spinster, surrounded by disgusting people just like yourself!" (OK, I gave in a little to the ugly side, so I'm not perfect... I know). Her reply was immediate, "That was not nice!" I volleyed back, "Don't ever contact me again!"

Shake, Rattle and Roll indeed!

Kenny G and Bobby at Steamboat Colorado. "Why'd ya beat me with that clarinet? I saw her first!"

Another situation that made me Shake, Rattle and Roll originated, again, from an earlier period in my life and played out in the present.

As I mentioned previously, while I was hustling toward my passion of comedy, I also worked in the garment industry. One of my main clients was this nice young lady. We had a solid rapport and even stayed in touch long after I left my Garmento life behind. As I climbed the ladder of comedy, this lady and her husband would come to most of my performances in the New York Tri-State Area. When the shows were over, and out of respect for my Garmento days, I'd make sure to stop by their table and say "Hi!"

On one occasion, Jill was at the club with me and as were walking away, she said, "Bobby, be careful! Those two are stalkers!" At the time, I didn't give much thought to her comment. And I'd almost forgotten about even seeing the two of them until, seemingly out of the blue the lady called me and asked, "Bobby, my husband has a business proposal he'd like to discuss with you. Do you mind if he calls you to set something up?" Not sure what to make of her request, I told her, "No problem."

A few days later, her husband reached out and asked if I could meet him and one of his old childhood friends at The National Arts Club (an old New York City establishment) for lunch. I agreed, and just to keep the sides even (not to mention, I had no idea what I might be walking into), I brought along one of my business friends to join the get-together. Over lunch, the husband and his friend inform me they want to open up a state-of-the-art comedy club in New York City.

When I heard this, I had no choice but to tell them, "The comedy market in New York City is already very crowded. What about Philadelphia or maybe Chicago? They're wide open. Neither city has a true comedy venue they can be proud of."

"No," they insisted. "New York City is *the* place."

So, I tried again. "This city already has two established 'headliner' comedy clubs and about eight other smaller 'showcase' clubs. Believe me, no *good* comic is going to jeopardize his/her relationship with the established clubs to jump to a new one, for *any* amount of money. Have you thought about Long Island? That might be a better market for you."

"No!" they practically shouted. "It's got to be in the City!"

"Well, then," I chuckled, "you'd better have deep pockets if you want to go up against the headliner clubs, because they're going to eat you up."

Simultaneously, they responded, "We *do,* and we're not worried."

Smiling at their response, I asked, "Why talk to me?"

"Because we've watched you perform for the last two years and you sell out everywhere you go. The other marquee headliner comics also hold you in high regard."

"Thank you," I told them. "But what's in it for me?"

They responded with an offer of 10% of the business.

Before I even realized it, I let out a laugh, "Oh, sorry, I didn't mean that," I told them with a smile. "But, I have to be honest, I'm not interested in being a shareholder. However, if you're asking me if I want to be a partner, that's a different story entirely."

You have to understand, I'm *old school*. A partnership to me means everyone has the same stake in the business, and since we're partners, we watch each other's back. Granted, there's always a risk of failure in any business, but it's the same risk across the board for everyone (this also means we equally share in any benefits). When we finished with lunch, I thanked them for their time before adding, "If you ever get your club up and running, give me a call."

Once we're out of earshot, my business friend turns to me and says, "Bobby, do you know who the husband's friend is? He's Joe Blow (for obvious reasons, I'm not using his real name). He's a big money player in the financial world. He's got a net worth of over a billion dollars!"

"Really?" I told my friend. "Well, he can't be very smart if he wants to go into a business he knows nothing about with just his open wallet in hand."

"Bobby, maybe you shouldn't be so hasty. You might want to think about this one."

"Nah, I'm going to take a pass."

Three weeks later, my LA lawyer, Tom (my business/investment lawyer, not to be confused with my basketball buddy attorney), called me and said, "What the hell did you do in that meeting with those guys in New York? Did you blow 'em?" I laughed (everyone is a comedian) and then told him the story. When I'm finished, Tom said, "Well, they just called me and want me to let you know the offer is now 30%." He goes on to tell me again (in monetary terms) exactly who these two New York City "big shots" are.

After listening closely, I told him, "Thirty percent of nothing is still nothing! They don't know comedy, and they've never run any type of club before! They don't have it. I looked into their eyes!"

He stopped me and told me to think for a second before

making a final decision. "Bobby, you've got to see the bigger picture here. This could be a nice addition to your portfolio, and if the club becomes a hit, it could be worth millions... and you would own 30%!"

After taking a few days to think things over, I called Tom back. "OK, I want you to go back to these guys and ask for an annuity."

"Are you crazy?" he responded.

"I have nothing to lose. Go and ask."

When Tom called back, he told me, "OK, they've agreed to pay you $75,000 per year, above and beyond your 30% ownership. This $75,000 will be broken down into payments of $6,250 per month. Happy now?"

Satisfied with their offer, I signed the deal. That's the SHAKE! Now here comes the RATTLE!

In order for me to receive my annuity, all three stipulations from our contract (listed below) must be met:

1) Find an established talent booker; someone who has good working relationships with not only comics, but with agents and managers to ensure he/she will be able to book top talent into the club
2) Invite other "headliners" (talent at the top of their game) to perform at the club
3) Work at the club no less than two times per year

My answers to these stipulations are summed up below:

1) No problem
2) I can ask, but knowing the strong loyalty comics develop over the years to established New York City clubs, I don't think they're going to simply toss this away to take a chance on a new, unproven venue. (Quite honestly, I don't

know if I would have jumped ship either if the situation were reversed, just because another comic asked me to)

3) Keeping in mind what I just said in #2, I'm going to have an annuity cushion that none of the other comics are going to have (which is why I can enter into this agreement). With that said, it's not going to be easy for me either. In order to take this shot, I will have to give up a long-established relationship with a club where I've performed for the past 18 years.

I felt completely confident the partners were going to put forth their best efforts to get the club up and running, but at the same time, I knew I needed to find a straight shooter for the job of talent booker. I needed someone who would act as my eyes and ears as to what's really going on at the club when I'm on the road working and who would guide the partners away from making too many mistakes, or at the very least, minimizing any trip-ups. Undoubtedly, this person should be schooled in all the inner-workings of a comedy club, including knowing how to handle any necessary payoffs in order to get the club set up. *Gasp! Did he just say payoffs? Oh, grow up, it's New York City!*

After a short period of time, the partners found a property to rent (not own), while I found a talent booker (who we'll call Patty) to start immediately. With Patty there to help put out any small brush fires and keep me in the loop as things progressed, the partners went about putting the club together. It turned out they were hell-bent on putting together a comedy club unlike any other in the country; definitely not your run-of-the-mill, stage-in-front, tables-around-the-room, microphone-on-the-stage club, but a $7,000,000 (seven MILLION dollar) state-of-the-art showpiece!

Now, I've worked at some very nice clubs (along with some real shitholes!), but I have to tell you, when I heard how much money they spent putting the club together, I couldn't imagine what they did to the space to result in a $7,000,000 bill! But when I talked to Patty, I started getting some insights. She told me they paid upwards of $400 for a single showroom chair, which in her experience is *insane!* Because as she or anyone with any sense for the club business knows, they can purchase 350 high-end commercial chairs from a restaurant liquidator or a used supply dealer or even a wholesale manufacturer for no more than $29 to $40 per chair. Seriously, $400 for ONE chair! They didn't get chairs; they got *thrones* (or ripped off big time!).

I eventually got to New York for my first visit to see the completed club, and as I walked through the front door, it's apparent that money meant nothing to these guys. The club was spectacular; it remains the *best* I've ever seen. Finding my way to the showroom, I naturally went to see what a $400 chair looks like, but I couldn't get a good look because the room was full of staff. I guesstimated there were at least sixty-four employees milling about, which is something I found interesting (and not in a good way) since the doors for the night didn't open for another three hours!

Once I found Patty, we made our way to the partners' office and, as we took our seats inside, I could see right away from the partners' body language the two of them were on one hell of an ego trip! I joked around for a few minutes, keeping the mood light – *little Bobby is working the kitchen table again* – but the whole time my mind was sifting through everything they'd done to the club. Finally, after getting a reassuring nod from Patty, I decided it was time for big Bobby – *the Bobby that's been in this business for a long time and knows it inside and out* – to speak. I didn't pull any punches. I began by letting loose with the question that'd been burning up my mind, "What the *hell* is going on here?"

One of them (I don't remember which) replied, "We're not sure what you mean, but it doesn't matter anyway, because what goes on here is basically none of your business."

"What are you talking about? I'm a partner in this club!" I shot back angrily. "And I know this business! As a matter of fact, Patty and I are the only ones in this room who have any idea how to run a club! You're at the starting line, just itching to take off, but you two have this place so top-heavy there's no way you're going to make it out of the block! You're setting yourself up to fail!"

Without so much as a blink of an eye, they repeated, "You have nothing to do with the operation of this club. How *we* run this club is no concern of yours."

I felt as if someone had punched me in the stomach. I left their offices disgusted and immediately called Jill to tell her what happened. "Stay away from them!" she told me. "They were just using you for bait! Watch, they're going to fall flat on their faces!"

Long after my trip to the club, Patty and I continued to talk and on one particular occasion, she said, "You wouldn't believe the astounding amounts of money the partners are telling me to offer comics just to get them booked into here. It's *stupid* numbers." She completely understood when I told her, "You know it's not going to take long for the other comics to catch wind of what you guys (meaning the partners) are paying. Everyone is just going to start asking for more and more money and pretty soon the club will have priced itself right out of the market."

The partners thought all they had to do was pay comics a lot more money than any of the other established New York City clubs and the comics would switch their allegiances to come work for them. WRONG! I knew what was going to happen *and it did*. Comics came and worked the club once (for the promised exorbitant fee), but never returned. This left the door wide open for other one-stop-shopping comics to come in and ask for even more money, forcing the club to keep paying out increasing amounts at an unsustainable rate.

Something else was happening, too. Comics would come over and ask me about the new club, knowing I was a partner. I would politely tell them (and anyone else for that matter), that I had moved on and was no longer associated with it. The chatter in the comedy community was, "Hey, why would Collins move on from such a beautiful club? Something

132

must not be kosher over there." Meanwhile, the other established clubs just stood by and laughed – waiting for the new club to implode – knowing that the minute it happened, the pay structure (that *they* created) would be reinstated. Sadly, some collateral damage was done to a few comics along the way, myself included. *Caroline's*, the club where I'd started out (and where I'd worked for 18 years), would no longer hire me because of my association with the new club. This caused me to lose my foothold in my original backyard: New York City.

The partners had sown their own seeds of destruction from the very beginning, which is what I tried to tell them (but they weren't interested in listening). Adding insult to injury, they stopped paying my annuity, citing failure to live up to our contractual agreement. I have to admit, this whole thing RATTLED me!

To settle up our differences, the partners and I went to court about six months later. Even though I'd lived up to everything I agreed to, I was still nervous. Once again, I was taking all of this as a *personal* attack, whereas the partners seemed to take everything in stride, treating our legal dispute as just another day at the office. So much so, that when we arrived at the courtroom, they tried to exchange friendly pleasantries with me! I was appalled! I wanted people like them whisked away from the planet!

My New York lawyer (not to be confused with my LA business/investment lawyer or my basketball buddy attorney) told me, "Today is merely the first step in their well-planned exit strategy. *Believe me,* this is definitely not their first time at the rodeo. They'll keep bringing you back into court until they exhaust all of your money or patience or both. They're betting you'll eventually decide enough is enough and walk away. All they're trying to do is outlast you."

Here's an important P.S. Back when my LA lawyer Tom was in negotiations with the partners regarding my contract, he very wisely included an arbitration clause. At the time, the partners told him any arbitration clause was going to be a deal-breaker. But when Tom relayed this information tome, I held firm, "Tell them, no arbitration clause, no contract." Eventually, they relented and agreed to leave in this clause exactly as Tom drafted it. They told him the main reason they changed their minds was because they thought if something ever does happen, Bobby would most likely just walk away. But they thought wrong! I'm a comic, and comics live by truths!

Needless to say, I had them beat hands down, with the court ruling to send my case to arbitration. When all was said and done, the partners were ordered to pay back all monies owed to me, in addition to my legal fees. They abided by this order for the next two months, but then abruptly stopped all payments. Unfortunately, by this time the 2008 recession was in full swing, which affected even the lawyers. I tried, but couldn't find anyone to take my case without money upfront, despite the fact it was a *surefire* winner. I needed to make a decision: Do I lay out $100,000 of my own money to go after them again, fully aware of the possibility that they could declare bankruptcy halfway through the proceedings, which would mean I would be left holding *yet another bag* (but this time a very expensive one!). This is what deep-pocketed businesspeople do – they suck the marrow out of the little guy and then whip out the bankruptcy flag and wave it all around right before they vanish into a distant memory. Of course, I could go with option #2: End this whole thing with a *c'est la vie* and just let it go.

After much discussion, Jill and I decided not to pursue the matter any further, feeling it was ultimately not worth the aggravation. Knowing that every dog has its day, I gracefully let the whole deal and everything associated with it go by the wayside. I even managed to thank God for the experience and the lessons learned:

        1) Always do your best to meet your creative needs
           and support your family
        2) Remember, when you grow as a person,
           change is inevitable

3) I was taking things too personally and the lesson to lighten up was very valuable, getting me ready for whatever was coming next

It turns out (much to my satisfaction) this dog had his day much sooner than expected. A local television station in New York City has a segment called *SHAME! SHAME! SHAME!* Each month they report on a despicable character, showing highlights of that person's wanton behavior toward mankind. They then see if they can get these creatures to explain themselves on the air. Well, guess what *Creature from the Black Lagoon* was a recent target? Yep, you guessed it – my billionaire partner from the comedy club. Outside his Park Avenue apartment, a reporter from the TV show confronted him. "You recently held a charity event at your comedy club. We'd like to know why you won't pay the $7,400 you promised them? Why would a billionaire welch on his promise and stiff such a respected and worthwhile charity?"

Ah, the smell of redemption... the ROLL!

I offer these stories to point out there is a lot of Shake, Rattle and Roll in *everyone's* life. Unfortunately, it's necessary in order for us to learn, grow and move on to the next level. Just remember, each level serves as a step to the next, with lessons revealed each time, lessons that only make you stronger and better prepared for *your* journey.

I say, "Bring it on!"

Chapter 10
CELEBRITY

I like to think that each one of us is a celebrity in our own right. We all have something special to offer. Over the years, I've met so many people that excel in life and are much more important than those people we call "celebrities." It's downright scary. So, just because someone isn't on TV, or in the movies, or written a book, doesn't make them any less special or important. In fact, in most cases, it makes them much *more* important.

I'm always amazed how fascinated people are with celebrity in this country. They think Brad Pitt is going to run into their burning house and save them one day! But I've seen and worked with so many of these celebrities... and you know what? I truly believe most of them are morons! If they couldn't remember the neatly typed lines on the pages handed to them, I don't know what else they would do for a living, because there's no way they could hold down a real job. They would constantly be in trouble with the law and truthfully, most of them actually are! Their conversations start with "I" and end with "me."

To make matters worse, we are inundated with the most trivial stories of these people on TV, online and in magazines, like we're supposed to care. Really, who gives a shit if Ashton Kutcher and Demi Moore are getting divorced? I didn't care when they got married, so why would I care now that they're going their separate ways? What I find really sad is too many people actually think this bullshit is important AND think they actually know these celebrities! But let's call it like it is. Did Michael Jackson's head look like a Pez dispenser? I sure think so. I used to turn on the TV and see him in his pajamas holding an umbrella – I'm from New York – to me that's *Mary Poppins*! OK, I know he's dead, but I wrote that before he died, so there...

As I said, I think *most* celebrities are morons, but there

are exceptions – so I'd like to namedrop a few of those exceptions here. Of course, I'd love to also share the names of those who wore the "moron sash," but I have to remember what my mother taught me, "If you can't say something nice, don't say anything at all!" I also don't want to wake up one morning and find a horse's head in my bed, or open my front door and have some twenty-year-old squeal out, "Daddy!"

I can tell you this: all *great* performers share a common thread (particularly the superstars), and that thread is simple: work extremely hard, act professionally and always treat *everyone* the Right Way.

I toured with Cher; what a classy lady. When you consider all her wig changes and costume changes, on top of her non-stop singing and *shake it 'til you break it* choreographed numbers,you can understand why people walk away from her shows knowing they just saw something special. Every night, I'd walk out on stage to open the show and I'd see an incredible cross-section of people. Folks, for whatever reason, were there because Cher had struck a chord in their lives. There were young kids who grew up hearing their parents sing *I Got You Babe* and *Gypsys, Tramps & Thieve;* or their mothers who admired her for succeeding as a woman in the male-dominated world of rock and roll. There were also plenty of all-American males who adored her and knew all the words to her songs (even if they would never admit it to their co-workers!). Not surprisingly, Cher also had a large following of gay supporters. Supporters who held her up as an icon for her strong over-the-top performances and willingness to accept anyone stepping out of a closet – *or a pantry!* To round things out, she also had a lot of older fans, people who grew up watching to her as one half of *The Sonny & Cher Comedy Hour*, who then continued to watch and support her as she went off on her own, developing into an award- winning actress.

Wait... "Jill, what's that Cher movie with Nicolas Cage? You know what I'm talking about, the Italian movie." "*Moonstruck.*"

"Yeah, *Moonstruck*, that's it!"

I also just saw that one again, with her and the girl who

Cher with Bobby before a show at Jones Beach Theater, Long Island, NY. "Was I supposed to dress up?"

got caught stealing...Oh, what's her name? Wynona Judd. No, that's not it.

"Hallie! What's that movie where Cher is the single mom, the town tramp, Wynona whatshername's the daughter..."

"Come on, Dad! For the tenth time, her name is Wynona Ryder and the movie you keep asking me about is *Mermaids*."

"Right... *Mermaids*."

See what happens when you get older? You have to rely on other people to remember for you. That's why you should always have younger and smarter people around you at all times!

People today still ask me what Cher is like. They have this image of her riding on the back of a Harley in her underwear, her arms wrapped around a younger guy, looking like she doesn't have a care in the world. Or they remember the tabloid covers showing the glammed-out Grammy Award-winning singer and TV star with some degrading headline splashed across the photo. See, the media doesn't care if it's true. They know human beings will always remember the negative press far more than the positive press because negativity sells!

That is why we rarely ever get to see the focused, hard-working professional Cher who, before *every* performance, gathers her people on stage to hold hands and say a prayer for the strength to deliver the best damned show they can for each and every person sitting in the audience. Telling her people, since everyone in the audience cares so much about us, they're willing to lay down their hard-earned cash to see us perform, they *deserve* to be royally entertained! The tabloids simply aren't interested in that caring human being, a true professional who "gets it": the *real* Cher.

In addition to touring with Cher, I also toured with sensual Spanish crooner, Julio Iglesias (Enrique's father). Boy, what a *great* guy! The women went nuts over him! Especially the women wearing those long dresses covered with little mirrors!

139

Julio taught me many things, but the most important thing was professionalism, which I learned the hard way.

We were working one night in Texas in this huge auditorium, and for whatever reason I didn't make sound check. Looking back, I probably didn't make it because as the sub-star, the second fiddle, I felt I would be overstepping my place to take the time to run a check, and I didn't want to do anything that could possibly result in my puny stage time running over into Julio's. After the doors opened to 20,000 paying customers, I went on stage and did my thirty-two minutes, but I could hear the sound wasn't right. It wasn't crisp, clear and sharp. To make matters worse, I finished up and left the stage without saying anything to Julio about it. When the show was over, Julio called me into his dressing room and let me have it!

"Bobby, you have to make sure your presentation is the best ever! It's your responsibility! If they have to hold the doors while you check the mike or whatever, so be it! Let them wait!"

What a valuable lesson he taught me that day. I'm no less than the "star;" I'm the master of my own show and it's my job to make sure I not only deliver my best, but check everything – including the equipment – so my best actually makes it to the people who've paid their hard- earned money to come see me perform! I've always been thankful for that lesson, and to this day I make sure the sound is right and the music is ready every time I step up on stage. You hang with the best, you become the best! Conversely, when you work with shit... *watch out!*

I've also opened for Dolly Parton, Tony Bennett, The Pointer Sisters, The Four Tops, Chicago, Henny Youngman, Kenny Loggins, Natalie Cole and many others. I've even been personally introduced back stage to show business legends, including Frank Sinatra, Dean Martin, Jerry Lewis, Rodney Dangerfield and Johnny Carson. When I started my comedy career in New York City, I worked alongside contemporaries such as: Chris Rock, Jerry Seinfeld, Kevin James, Ray Romano, Drew Carey, Tim Allen, Jay Leno, Howie Mandel, Eddie Murphy, Rita Rudner, George Wallace, Garry Shandling, Louie Anderson, Paul Reiser, Rosie O'Donnell, Carrot Top.

Julio Iglesias and Bobby, Caesar's Palace. "Yo, Julio – I'm married, brother!"

Throughout my entire career I've worked with a host of other outstanding comics, who may be less known to the public, but are in no way less talented!

I admire and respect any hard-working, talented professional, no matter what their occupation is. Which is why I have to ask you, if you watch *The Real Housewives of New York City* or buy *People* magazine to read about Charlie Sheen, Lindsay Lohan, Britney Spears or the Kardashians, to please keep it in perspective.

I can hear someone say, "Who cares if Kim Kardashian is an idiot! She's rich!" My argument is the same as it was before; "I'd rather be poor, happy and smart, than rich and stupid!"

That's the difference now – the vast majority of today's "celebrities" want the adulation from everyone for simply *being*. Not for anything they've actually accomplished, which may contribute positively to another person or principle, but for doing *nothing*. They simply fail to exhibit the slightest notion of responsibility for themselves or the consequences of their actions. It's like they have no realization of their disconnection from normal society. This is not to say that all celebrities are simply an 8 x 10 glossy, because there are many who are accomplished at their craft and use their fame (and money) for worthy causes. However, it seems more and more like the *surreal* are overtaking the real!

People, do yourself a favor – picture your own face on that magazine cover or imagine being interviewed on the red carpet. See yourself as the celebrity that you are! And please, if you're one of those who believe Ramona from *The Real Housewives of New York City* or Teresa from *The Real Housewives of New Jersey* exemplifies strength and independence, admit you've been standing too close to the microwave while you cook! All those "housewives" are nothing more than social climbers, using the men and other women in their lives to play out their uniquely classy drama as genuinely as a WWE wrestling match. I know classy women, and these women are no Jackie O! If anything, they represent the lowest common denominator in our society, albeit wearing expensive shoes and promoting bad hair!

Even if you're smart enough to know this already, you still might know someone who wouldn't dream of missing a single episode of *The Real Housewives, Jersey Shore, Dancing With the Stars, The Biggest Loser, Keeping Up with the Kardashians, Survivor, So You Can Think You Can Dance* (which I can), or *blah, blah, blah,* just to feel better about

Paul Reiser, Kelly Carlin, and Bobby, The Comedy & Magic Club, Hermosa Beach, California, at a birthday tribute for George Carlin. "'Nuff said."

themselves. Do them a favor and help them select a small room in their house to hang themselves.

I can't be the only person who is hoping that somewhere there's a dickwad of a producer or television executive with the gonads or ovaries (even if it's only to save their job from extinction) that's about to have his/her "Eureka!" moment. *If we keep making everyone a reality star, pretty soon there won't be anyone at home to watch television!* Seriously, someone has to step up and bring back the writers, writers who use the art of words to tell stories. It doesn't matter if they are funny stories, stories of hope, or even stories filled with sadness, just as long as they stretch our imaginations and encourage us to think and relate to something (or someone) of merit.

But everyone with a television set must also take some responsibility too, which is actually quite simple. Here's a quick 101 on how television works. Networks run TV shows. Networks are run by money. This money comes from advertisers. The more people who watch a TV show, the more a network can charge for advertising. So, when a TV show isn't watched, the advertisements don't get seen, which makes the advertisers believe their products aren't going to be purchased and the money dries up. The end result is the network dumps the show.

So you see, we as viewers aren't as powerless to demand that networks raise the bar on their programming as you might've first thought. But once again, it's going to take more than just talking the talk. Merely complaining about the sorry state of television doesn't do squat! You have a powerful tool in the palm of your hand, but you have to use it! The next time, and *every* time, you land on one of these crappy TV shows trying to pass as entertainment – CHANGE THE CHANNEL! TURN THAT SHIT OFF! If everyone did this, you can bet the message would be heard loud and clear!

But bad television isn't something new. When I was a kid, my father used to tell me, "You keep watching that idiot box (television) and you'll wind up stupid." Well, over the years, there were many times after sitting cross-legged, zoned-

144

out, in front of the boob tube before going to bed when I'd wake up the next morning and find brain matter stuck to my pillow! But the problem now is there are a lot more than just three networks, which has only multiplied the poundage of bad TV!

Recently, I was passing through the living room when I caught Hallie watching that moronic *Jersey Shore*. Sitting down next to her, I asked, "What are you doing?"

"Dad, they're just *so* dumb," she tells me.

"Well, you're watching them, so what's that say about you?"

"Whadaya mean?"

"Hallie, they can't help being dumb. All they're doing is allowing everyone just to see how dumb they are."

"Yeah, but they're getting a buttload of money to do it!"

"Money isn't everything, you know this. Besides, what happens when they no longer have a TV show?"

"They'll be rich!"

"Wrong! They'll *still* be dumb."

It's time to call it like it is – television is dumbing down America! Don't empower DUMB! We can no longer simply ignore that our kids will soon be too dumb to know the difference between what is acceptable and bad behavior. 'Cause I'm telling you, right now, what they're learning is, it doesn't matter what you do or how you behave toward another person, just as long as it makes YOU money... "It's all good!"

It's up to each of us to teach our children and show them by example what is acceptable and what is not – *not those reality idiots!*

I've worked in films, been in TV commercials and performed on stage, and the way entertainers are treated is amazing! Your every need is catered to: clothes, food, transportation, hotel, trailer... *and don't forget the big salaries!* So it's not too hard to understand how any celebrity, who maybe not that long ago was a struggling actor just trying to make their rent, can get used to this treatment. And why not? It

145

definitely beats standing in line for food stamps or having to deal with the Department of Motor Vehicles (DMV) where they treat you like chopped meat!

What celebrities need to remember is *nothing* lasts forever. There will come a day when they are no longer famous and people won't remember who they are (or they simply won't be relevant to the world around them anymore), and that's when the problems begin. When bygone stars get testy and do something stupid, you and I read about them or see them on TV and not in a good way!

I guess, the point I want to make is this: there's nothing wrong with showing appreciation to a performer (including comics) or enjoying your favorite movie star (up to a point), but no one should ever be envious of celebrities. I know you wish you could do what they do, to have what you perceive to be their life, but the truth is you probably couldn't do what they do. T*hat's not your path!* (Just like they probably could never do what you do).

Like I said in the beginning, we are each on our own journey, and one path is no more or less important than any other. Bottom line: everyone is a "celebrity" in their own world, which is why I can tell you it doesn't matter to me if the celebrities I know star in blockbuster movies or reels of summer vacations. I'm proud to call all of them my friends.

Bobby and Darrell Hammond at The Comedy Cellar, New York, New York. "You're wearing your Goth tonight? Me, too!"

Chapter 11
OF THE PEOPLE, BY THE PEOPLE, FOR THE PEOPLE...YEAH, RIGHT!

I PREDICT FUTURE HAPPINESS FOR AMERICANS IF THEY CAN PREVENT THE GOVERNMENT FROM WASTING THE LABORS OF THE PEOPLE UNDER THE PRETENSE OF TAKING CARE OF THEM.
—Thomas Jefferson

This brings me to my next observation: today's politicians are either the best or the worst (depending on your viewpoint) reality stars of all. Washington, D.C., has become the stage for the Dewey, Cheatem & Howe show. I'm telling you, the cable guy is more reliable (and trustworthy) than the government. How about those poor people in New Orleans? They were waiting for the government to rescue them... the government! The government can't even hand out cheese right. There are *still* people standing on street corners in the Bronx asking strangers, "Hey! You want some Velveeta?"

The best any of us can do is pay our taxes, wear a helmet and stay low!

OF THE PEOPLE: What are we lacking as a people if today's "leaders" are the best we can offer up? I was always taught in school that our government was set up to lead, look out for and be responsive to *all* of us, AND if that government isn't, we have the responsibility and the right to install one that is! Our government has been put up for sale. The lobbyists are the brokers and we're all suffering the consequences. If it wasn't for sports or television, we'd all be down in our basements right now cleaning out our muskets, thinking of ways to overthrow the government. Look around people – if you don't think it can happen here, keep wiping out the middle class and watch what happens!

I realize the world is now all one big global economy, with an interdependence of nations, but it wasn't that long ago there actually were REAL Mr. Smiths going to Washington. Today, we watch the *Ides of March* and have no trouble recognizing the "fictional" characters! No one seems particularly incensed by the everyday tales of political "goings on." The reality is, we've become a caricature of ourselves. Small radical extremist countries are using what we've done to them over the years and are now throwing it back into our faces with a vengeance... and we don't like it! I think it's time we get back on where we got off! We're playing a dangerous game of *I'm going to make myself better at your expense.* It sets a bad example. Whatever happened to keeping it simple? There's a thin line between loyalty and dissent, and I thought our country was based on dissent – the Boston Tea Party, the American Revolution, the First Amendment, Vietnam War protests, etc. I also always liked the fact that we could speak our minds without fear of being accused of being anti-American. It allowed "We the People" to play a pivotal role in that whole checks and balances thing.

I suppose politics follows the same adage as everything else – there's my way of thinking, your way of thinking and then there's the Right Way. Right now, American politicians seem to be dead set on MY way, *way too much.* Case in point, the color of our president's skin is STILL a topic of discussion (some just camouflage it more than others). Personally, I don't care if we have a purple president; if he can get everyone working together and get us out of the mess we're in, he's my guy! Besides, I thought we were done with that whole racism thing. Oh, excuse me, I was applying wisdom where ignorance reigns supreme. My bad!

There seems to be a pot of gold out there (probably from our tax money), and these people we call politicians are lying, cheating and doing everything they can to steal it from each other. But, of course, it's all "for the good of the people!" Was it for "the good of the people" when the survivors of Hurricane Katrina (a vast majority lacking personal transportation) responded to the question of why they didn't just leave New Orleans, with an answer of, "We were waiting for the government!" Or was it for "the good of the people"

149

when they were waiting on the rooftops of their homes or looking for someone to help clean up the bodies floating down the streets? The truth is, our government failed to deliver on so many levels during the Hurricane Katrina crisis, and even today, fails to provide "for the good of the people" of New Orleans.

Turn on the television and you'll see our politicians going face-to-face in a pissing match over the debt crisis, with a non-stop parade of agencies blaming other agencies – bureaucrats accusing other bureaucrats. When this happens, who's left to assign accountability and render justice? That's right, *we* are! Politicians can no longer afford to see us as "the masses are the asses," just as we can no long afford to see politicians as "the crusaders and guardians of truth and justice. Our eyes have been opened! I *know* they have. We can't blindly trust our elected officials anymore. *Trust can no longer be a given; politicians must earn it.* Every elected official, from small town councilmen to the President of the United States must, by their actions and reactions, prove they are acting in our best interest. They must demonstrate to each of us they have a heart, a soul and a conscience!

Can you imagine working for a company that has a little more than 500 employees, and among them one has posted numerous pictures of his dick, another is caught in a pubic bathroom soliciting other men for blowjobs, one in Florida is propositioning interns for sex, and the CEO uses cigars to fulfill some inner, twisted, sexual fantasy!

These are the idiots who we've elected to crank out hundreds of laws each year designed to keep the rest of us in line. People, wear a helmet, pay your taxes and stay low!

BY THE PEOPLE: We're fighting two wars in lands where the people have no hope. Hasn't even *one* of these politicians ever played basketball in the inner city? You never go up against people who have no hope. They have nothing to lose! They *always* win!

I live in California. Arnold Schwarzenegger used to be my governor. People thought he was a real governor. He was

150

an actor playing the part of a governor! But, I have to admit, it was a bit refreshing to know the population of California had broken away from the national herd, dismissing typical politicians and then surprising everyone, probably even Arnold himself (and most definitely Maria!) by electing an ACTOR to be our governor. But really, what were we thinking? OK, so Arnold wasn't the first actor to become a politician, and I don't care what you thought about Ronald Reagan one way or the other – the fact is the man could speak. He knew how to reach an audience with language. But THIS actor? There's a reason why the directors never gave him too many lines in his movies... "I'll be back!" "And CUT!"

How about the ex-Governor of New York, David Paterson? He was trying to hustle twenty Yankee tickets so he could attend a game with his people. But here's the real kicker – *he's blind!* Why not just take him to a Little League game! Give him a play-by-play if you want, "Hey Governor, did you bring your mitt? Jeter just hit one out of the park... Yeaaaaaaahhh! Governor, want some more popcorn?" Please!

Let's not forget about Elliot Spitzer, the governor of New York before David Paterson. The one who was paying hookers thousands of dollars a night *for years* before he finally got caught. Talk about an expensive habit to kick! After he was forced out of office, take a guess where he landed from his fall from grace? That's right... on television! With his own show and a new law firm, Spitzer, Swallow and Come! Only in America, people!

FOR THE PEOPLE: A while back, I was sitting in my office when I received a phone call for a potential gig. "Mr. Collins, some colleagues and I recently saw you in Las Vegas. We'd like to know if you would be interested in a private performance in Austin, Texas, for about 750 people."

"I'm listening," I responded with a chuckle.

The lady on the other end went on to give me the date she was interested in, but before we could agree on a price, she asked, "Do you have any reservations about working for an Intelligence Organization?"

151

"By intelligence, do you mean a brotherhood of brainiacs or the government?"

"The government," she said, laughing.

"No problem," I answered. "People discriminate; money doesn't."

With a signed contract (my own) faxed over a few days later, I found myself stepping off a plane in Austin, where I was greeted by a bunch of serious-looking guys in dark suits, each wearing those little mouthpiece/headphone things on their cheeks. They immediately whisked me away in a black Cadillac Escalade, which I somehow know is in lock-down mode. They escorted me all the way to my hotel room door, where the head suit told me, "Do *not* leave this room for any reason. Someone will be here to walk you down to your show."

Back when I secured this gig, I called my comic friend Mike, who lives in Austin. I told him the date, location and time, and then asked him to come to the show. I often do this (contact friends in destination cities where I know I'm going to be performing and invite them to my shows) since it not only helps ensure there is a friendly face in the crowd, but it also allows me to stay connected with old friends. However, since this was a private function, I can only give Mike the phone number I'd been given for a guest to be added to my "list."

Now, a few hours after my arrival, as the "men in black" are about to escort me from my hotel room to the show, I turned to the head suit (since he seemed to know everything that was going on) and said, "Before I forget, did my friend Mike get his name added to the list OK?"

"Sorry, your friend failed to pass our background check. He wasn't cleared. He will *not* be attending the event this evening."

"Ah, OK, sure. Well, that takes care of that then..." was all I could stammer back. *Shit, I would've loved to have heard that whole conversation!*

Since my curiosity was now *killing* me, I had to ask one more question before we stepped into the hall, "OK, so who am I performing for tonight?"

The head suit looked at me and without even a hint of

sarcasm, responded, "Homeland Security, the FBI and the CIA."

This response sent a shiver down my spine, because if anything happened to the people in that room, the whole intelligence network of the United States could go down like a house of cards! *But what could I say back to him?*

"Can I talk about this administration?" I finally asked. "Administrations come and go; *we're* always going to be here."

"Good answer," I shot back with a smile.

I went out that night and performed... and you know what? I had a ball! The room was filled with wonderful, wonderful people. Afterwards, a group of them offered to take me out to dinner. So naturally, I asked, "Hey, if I wasn't any good, would you still be taking me out to dinner?"

The head suit looked at me again with that serious, Secret Squirrel, government-agent look, the one that makes you wonder if they're reading anything diabolical into what you just said.

"Right."

So, there I was at the restaurant, wearing my usual stage clothes – black shirt and black dress pants – sitting with this group of Xeroxed, blue-suit wearing, serious-faced government agents. I could see the thought bubbles hanging above the heads of everyone else in the restaurant – *It looks like they've finally found Waldo!* Hey, don't get me wrong, thank God people like this exist. I just don't normally roll with them on an everyday basis!

After the appetizers came, I looked across the table and asked, "So, you can't all be named Chip and Oscar. What are your real names?"

"Chip and Oscar will do just fine," they responded without as much as a grin.

Eventually, I get them to loosen up a little (remember, I'm from New York; we're always looking to score a free get out of jail card!) and once we really started to enjoy ourselves, I couldn't help but ask, "You guys ever just go out and party? You know, let yourselves get all wild and crazy?"

153

FBI Chip responds, "Like you did in 1972 at the University of Buffalo?" (I got into an altercation with a student security guard on campus, which I had to go to court to settle. The whole thing turned out to be harmless). My mouth dropped!

"They didn't even have computers back then," I told him. "Those files were probably locked away in some basement somewhere."

CIA Oscar replies, "Don't worry, we have those files."

Our dinner continued, and actually became an enjoyable night out with a bunch of guys. One of the agents, who was more personable than the others (we've remained friends), said sometime during dinner, "Bobby, you of all people should know that most people don't want to see their life without rose-colored glasses on. They don't want to see, much less acknowledge, that 7 out of 10 people are in debt, 2 out of 4 people have a police record, and 1 out of 2 people are on some type of medication." He went on to say, "Or that most bank robbers get away with it (which somehow I knew). We only publicize the ones who get caught, to discourage other people from trying to rob more banks."

That conversation – in fact, everything about that day's events – pointed out something very important to me. I thought I saw our country, and life, pretty clearly, but I'm a rookie compared to my friend at the FBI.

Things aren't the way they should be. It's like we're all supposed to follow this blueprint for the made-up world we're living in: work hard, take out a mortgage (or two), have 2.3 children (I never understood the fraction of a child thing), pay your taxes (cheat a little), scrimp and save to go on vacation, get in trouble with the law twice in your lifetime (traffic or something else minor) and BE HAPPY with your debts, stress level and gerbil wheel existence! Because once you buck the system... they'll try to step in and remove you!

I remember John Lennon used to say just keep them drugged with TV and sports, and make sure to always create crises to keep the masses occupied (gas prices, war, immigration, same-sex marriage), so the rich can get richer and pay less and less taxes, while the middle class pays all the taxes, leaving the lower class to claw its way up and battle it out with the middle class for what's left. It's a perfect numbing/dumbing system. Everyone is occupied with scrambling around doing what's been set up for them to do, instead of stopping and looking at what's really going on. It's like we're all children and there's this big parent that's always watching to make sure we're staying in line. But don't you just want to scream at them sometimes, "Hey, stop it!" Forget about *The Da Vinci Code*; how about we overhaul and rejuvenate *The American Dream Code?*

It's your right and duty to question everything! Don't get caught up in your own daily snapshot – see the whole picture! Because that's the only way you'll be able to process the idea that 99% of what we don't see is reality, and the 1% that we do see (and where you and I actually live) is nothing more than bullshit!

So what's the average Joe to do? I repeat... *wear a helmet, pay your taxes and stay low!*

Joe Montana and Bobby, Harrah's Lake Tahoe. "Hey, Joe, go long!"

Chapter 12
YOU CAN'T LOSE WHAT YOU NEVER HAD

I recently played basketball with some friends, and upon leaving, I talked to a guy named Lee, who I hadn't seen in a while.

"So, how's it going, Lee-man?"

"I'm working a lot of freelance, which is good. But personally, it's been a little rough lately."

"Second marriage?"

"Yeah, Bobby. She's crazy! I would say it's 50/50 right now."

If a guy tells me his woman is crazy, I can understand it. As a matter of fact, whatever happened to crazy? Crazy doesn't get the respect it once did. Crazy always worked for me – I grew up with crazy. Everyone knows the rules on crazy: you ignore crazy unless it touches you, and then you have permission to kill crazy!

I know plenty of guys just like Lee. They'd get married, and then I wouldn't see them for a few years, and when I did, their answer to my question, "How's the marriage going?" was simply, "She went crazy!"

You know what? That's enough for me! No more explanations needed. I don't need the stories. "She put the cat in the blender..." Stop! It's OK, I understand. Really, that's all I needed to hear. She went crazy; the relationship had to end right there!

Anyway, back to my friend Lee. As we reached our cars, I asked, "What happened?"

He proceeded to tell me his wife has a hang-up about financial security. Before the two of them got married, they talked about starting a family together. But now that they're two years in, she feels they aren't financially secure enough to provide for themselves and someone else, even with his freelancing jobs (which, by the way, he does very well with – remember, this is the entertainment business) and her working full-time, seven days a week.

"Isn't this exactly the same work set-up as before you got married?" I asked.

"Yes," he replied, "but she has these deep-rooted insecurities about how her father failed to provide for her growing up. It's so deep in there, I'm not sure if she can work it out. That's why it's 50/50."

"You can't lose what you never had," I said.

"Yeah, I think you might be right, Bobby."

I'm a firm believer that if something is meant to be, it will be! Call it karma, fate, luck, or whatever; I just believe things happen for a reason. You can try and stick a square peg in a round hole and hope for the best, but if things don't work out, you have to learn to see the situation for what it is and move on.

I'm also a firm believer that there is someone out there for everyone. But this person isn't going to knock on your door and say, "Hey, it's me! I've been waiting for you!"

We're all here for a blink of an eye. Love, happiness, sharing, giving, and intimacy – everyone deserves these – but remember, you have to do the work!

Another friend of mine, who's been married for twenty-two years, recently called me up and said, "Donna and I are divorcing."

Now, I know "opposites attract," but I remember being at their wedding and thinking, *He has a huge personality, but very little ambition. Donna is quiet, reserved, fearful of his friends, too controlling, blah, blah, blah. So, what the hell is this guy doing? Why would he select this type of woman to marry?*

Hey, don't get me wrong, I felt bad for my friend. Divorce is tough. Whether you're married for two years or twenty-two years, it *hurts*. It's difficult handling everything the Right Way, particularly if kids are involved. But talking with kids honestly about what's going on, and removing all the blame (telling it like it is), generally is the Right Way to go. Because the truth is, kids always know what's going on anyway, and anything short of age-appropriate facts only confuses them! I can look into a kid's eyes and see whether a divorce was handled the Right Way, because when it's not, I can see the damage done... and it breaks my heart! I just want to smack the parents for being so self-absorbed they didn't bother to consider what effect their selfishness would have on their own children!

So, when I hear my friend Lee's relationship is hitting rocky times, or my friend's long marriage is ending, my response to each of them is the same, "You can't lose what you never had." *If it's meant to be, it will be!* If it comes back to you, great! But if it doesn't, *that's OK, too!* Life is too short to wallow in the *what ifs*, *should haves* and *could haves*. MOVE ON! Don't dwell on a snapshot from the past. See the bigger picture and find happiness!

Sometimes I wonder if a lack of honesty from the very beginning isn't the real problem with the majority of relationships. There's nothing sadder than seeing two people together that aren't happy, but play up their relationship to everyone else like they have the world by the balls! When really, if they were just honest with themselves, or the other person, from the start, they would have each kept looking to find the happiness they were meant to find instead of what was convenient at the time!

Maddie has this tutor – nice girl, twenty-six years old, smart, scored high on her SAT's, attractive and involved in an improvisational comedy group. Jill, of course, dragged me to see one of her shows, and you know what, this girl was great! She has some potential, a real diamond-in-the-rough.

One day, she and I were talking, and it was clear to me something was bothering her. "What's up?" I asked.

She felt comfortable enough to tell me, "This guy I've been seeing for about a month just broke it off."

"Why?"

"He's moving to New York to work on a TV show and doesn't want to take it any further."

OK, so here's how I interpret this last sentence: He doesn't want to see her anymore and doesn't want to hurt her –

158

cool, I'm good with that. But if you really want to look at it, he's just not ready yet for a serious relationship because (as we all know), you *can* have your cake and eat it, too! Or maybe he's just not telling this girl the real reason; that there's something about her personality that he doesn't like and he wants to move on. People think they're being kind by telling the other person the timing just isn't right, but the problem with that excuse is no one learns anything. A guy who does this is taking the easy way out by not telling the woman something she might want to improve upon, something she might want to change about herself. Or maybe it's just the opposite. Maybe the guy sees something in himself that he doesn't like, but has decided not to look at it right now (with guys, it's usually fear). So, the truth gets lost somewhere in the mix and the woman winds up dealing with it on her own, more often than not, wrongly blaming herself. *How come not me? I have all this to offer and he doesn't want any part of me? There must be something wrong with me.* So, here again, nothing gets resolved, yet both are moving on.

In my own life, I always liked when the person told me what that they didn't like about me, or why the situation wasn't working out. Many times, this person revealed that I was too much to handle, or they couldn't keep up with me. But you know what? Thank God! Not only did I appreciate the constructive criticism, I would never want to carry the weight of two people in a relationship! So the way I look at it, I never lost anything I didn't have.

And Maddie's tutor, I think she finally came to the same conclusion – if someone doesn't want to be with me, well, that's his loss! That's not to say you shouldn't take a look and see where you can improve yourself by making a change (or not) when the opportunity presents itself. But generally speaking, when you look, you'll see something, adjust it and then move on. At the same time, you have to be careful, because if you dwell too much on the past, you'll prevent yourself from living in the present. And if you're not living in the present, you'll more than likely miss what's right in front of you, what God has in store *right* around the corner.

Things happen for a reason – you can't lose what you never had!

My goddaughter applied to Oxford University in England. She was hoping to be one of only thirty-five American students accepted. (*When I was her age, I was hoping I could use community service on my application just to get in to a good junior college!*) After I learned she didn't get in, I called and left her the following message, "I'm so sorry. I know you're disappointed, but remember, you can't lose what you never had. If it was meant to be, they'll call back, and if not, move on. It wasn't in the cards. Someday, you'll look back and see why you weren't meant to go there, and you'll just smile, realizing you headed in the direction you were *meant* to go!"

By now, you're probably a little (or *a lot*) tired of seeing the phrase, "You can't lose what you never had." To be honest, I'm a little tired of typing it myself!

But you have to understand, I've seen too many people get the life sucked out of them simply because they never had control of their life to begin with. They failed to grasp this very simple, logical concept (last time, I promise!): You can't lose what you never had!

Chapter 13
TIDBIT RULES, YET IMPORTANT RULES NONETHELESS

Some things we only do in the privacy of our own home. Here's one: Never get out of the shower to pee! Why? You could possibly slip and hurt yourself! Granted you might have a fleeting worry of political correctness (along with a slight sanitary concern) that first time. But in truth, you can pee in the shower– no one cares! It all goes down the drain! Besides, the water keeps falling in the shower where it *all* gets carried away to be filtered and processed back into clean water. I also like to do it because I feel like I'm getting away with something a little naughty, while providing a satisfying, completely private, feeling of relief. Oh, come on! You know what I'm talking about!

And don't even tell me you've never had an eargasm! You know, when you tenderly insert a cotton Q-Tip into your ear (or the ear of your significant other), probing around until you hit just the right spot! You then lovingly twirl the Q-Tip around and around while the blood rushes into your ear canal, making the whole area warm and inviting, until your eyes flutter and roll into the back of your head! Wait, excuse me a minute... ahhhh, better ... OK, I'm back. Where was I? Oh yeah, you would never think of turning to your wife while you're in the health and beauty aisle of the store, and say, "Why don't you pull out a Q-Tip and let's get a little eargasm going, you dirty girl." No, because just like never getting out of the shower to pee, *some things we only do in the privacy of our own home.*

Here's another good tidbit rule to live by, although granted, as you mature, you find less of a need to evoke this rule, but occasionally, you still find it necessary: *Passengers always have executive power over a dumbshit driver.*

Remember in high school or college, you and your friends would all pile into one person's car to go out for the night? You'd all be at a club or some party, miles from home, and it would always be the driver who'd gather everyone in the corner and say, "Hey guys, I'm telling you, this girl is *special!* She just might be the one! I'm gonna take her home; you guys are on your own to find a ride."

WRONG!

Rule is: You take his keys and ask, "Where do we pick you up tomorrow?" The rest of you are now free to "tool around" for the remainder of the night – in his car!

Another similar situation is when you're out with friends and the driver proceeds to get shitfaced drunk at the first stop, then stubbornly refuses to hand over his keys. By Rule, you're allowed to take his keys and throw him into the trunk of his *own* car! Is he going to be pissed off? You bet he is! But you know what? Who cares? The next day, after he's sobered up, the only explanation he's due is the one that reminds him of the Rule.

I remember one time we had to throw Stevie into the trunk of his car, and on our way home, we got pulled over for having a taillight out. As we stood next to the police officer at the back of the car (this was when cops were more Andy Taylor than Dirty Harry), Stevie started kicking the inside of the trunk, screaming and yelling in tongues! So naturally the police officer orders us to open up the trunk. He takes one look (and whiff) of Stevie (of course, we're all thinking, *Oh shit! We're going to jail! He probably thinks we're kidnappers... or worse!*) and then I swear, he smiled and calmly closed the trunk. As he's writing in his booklet, he says, "I'm just gonna give you boys a warning this time. But you need to get this thing home right now and take care of it." Even today, I'm not sure if he was talking about the taillight or Stevie! Although I do like to think that even public servants are familiar with and respect the Rule.

Here's another tidbit rule that is actually a natural evolution of the preceding Rule: *Always take your own car.*

I'm down in Florida doing a show, and I have the family with me. We're having a good time, even though it's Florida in July. It's not just hot, it's Africa hot! I'm talking

162

Sahara, walk on the sun hot! You could buy T-shirts with wet armpits! I farted and my underwear ignited! Do you know how embarrassing it is to have to call a fire truck to put your ass out in public?

Sorry, back to my story. So I'm down in Florida with the family and I get a call from my friend Kerry. Kerry is a good guy and a good friend. He invites all of us to a concert by some European group called Il Divo. All this means to me is five guys singing in a foreign language, which also means there's no way for me to know if any of them makes a mistake! As we're talking, Kerry says, "To make things easy, I'll pick all of you up in my Escalade."

"Why such a big car?" I ask.

"It's for the kids."

I'm thinking, *if you have kids that big, cut them in half!* But instead, I say, "You know what, why don't I just rent a car and we'll meet you there" – because you *always take your own car!*

"No way!" Kerry tells me. "Not only are our seats great, but I also got us gold parking passes. This thing is going to be packed. You'll never get parking like this. It'd be stupid for all of us not to go together." While my brain is still saying, *Always take your own car,* my mouth says, "If that's the case... uh, sure, OK. Come pick us up."

Hours later, we all pile into Kerry's Escalade and go to the concert, which turned out to be great! We enjoyed ourselves immensely! When the group is just about done with its last number, I give Kerry "the look." You know, "the look" that says, *OK, this thing is almost over. If we leave right now, we can get to the car and beat the traffic out of here and still remember this night as fun!*

Message received. He's just about to stand up when some people come over to him and start talking ... and talking... and talking.

See, the thing about being married to someone for a long time is they can read your mind! I hadn't said a word, cracked a joke, or even flexed to deliver an elbow nudge when Jill looks at me and commands without uttering a sound, *Bobby, be patient. These are Kerry's friends. Let him speak to them.*

Finally, the show ends and everyone is being herded toward the exits. Only now, these "pretty, talky people" have entered our orbit and are moving right along with us. Mind you, they're still yapping away to Kerry the whole time. That's when he says something that catches my ear, "Hey, no problem. You can ride with us."

What? Is he nuts? Surely he's noticed during our trudge across the asphalt frying pan that my hair has melted and is now sliding off my head! Not to mention sweat has dripped into my right eye, which has caused it to pop out, so all that's left is a slinky hanging down from the socket! Just maybe, if I attach a flare to it, he'll notice how it's bouncing up and down with each step... and then he'll get the message! No new passengers! Sorry! This bus is full and leaving right now!

Only when Kerry says to me, "Hey. Bobby, you guys go to the car. I'll be right there," do I realize we're totally screwed!

So off we go, Jill, the girls and me to find the car and wait for Kerry. Of course, it isn't until we actually get to his mammoth motor vehicle that I realize we don't have the key. Not wasting a second, I take my wallet and driver's license out and start holding it over my head.

"What are you doing?" Jill asks, totally confused.

"I'm getting ready," I tell her. "This way, when someone finally finds us, they'll at least be able to put a name to one of the four puddles with eyeballs!"

Jill doesn't say a word back to me; she just gives me another one of her "looks."

So, there we are, the four of us, standing... and waiting... and waiting... in the middle of this steaming asphalt parking lot for Kerry to come back to his car. I practically check my cell phone every second for any sign from Kerry, but there are no service bars. I can't even call 911! I turn around and Jill is growing a beard! A few minutes later, a day bus packed with fossils towing a pile of aluminum walkers goes by. A few minutes after that, I watch as the parking attendants wave goodbye to us after they finish counting the receipts for the night, put the "closed" sign up and zoom away. But still, no Kerry!

Finally, on the horizon, across the black expanse, I see three mirage-like figures approaching us with heat waves rising all around them. "Sorry, guys," Kerry says as he and his two friends come into focus. "I forgot where we parked. We wound up walking over to the opposite side of the stadium. Hope the wait didn't get too hot for you."

Luckily, I don't carry a knife. *Always take your own car.*

Here's the thing: not all tidbit rules involve hygiene or transportation, and this one should never be forgotten: *Never go back to a party you just left.*

Why? Because it's never the same party by the time you get back. I can't tell you how many times (in the old days), when I'd be out with a dud of a girl at a party, I'd find myself, thinking, *If I can just lose this dead weight, there are at least two or three other possibilities waiting for me right here!* Of course, I'd stay with the dud (because I'm a gentleman), but the minute I dropped her off, I'd tear back to the party hoping to pick up on the vibe I'd left behind.

Without fail, on my way back to the party, I always envisioned it being as hot as it was when I was standing there with Lassie, feeling sorry for myself and being envious of everyone else laughing, whooping it up and shouting, "Koo! Koo! Koo!" or whatever they were hollering! As soon as I walked back into the party, all revved up and ready to finally get down with my "bad self," the door would open up to *The Twilight Zone!* There was never any more whooping, laughing and fun. Did someone die? Was there a suicide bomber? What happened to the music? And where did that girl with the boobs so big you could chip a tooth on them run off to? Call it just reward, a shift in parallel time, fate or whatever, but it was *never* the same party!

I'll admit, it took me a couple Rod Serling episodes before I finally filed those nights into my mental hard drive so they'd automatically replay whenever I caught myself thinking,

Ten minutes until I can drop her off! Ten minutes until I can come back to this party and really go nuts!

Trust me on this one – *Never go back to a party you just left.* Very good rule.

OK, I debated this next rule *a lot.* Because it's really more than a tidbit rule, yet not enough that I'd categorize it as a life lesson (but it's close!). So I settled on calling it a Golden Tidbit Rule: *Never get back with an old girlfriend or wife* (of course, this is equally true for women; it's just that I'm a guy, so naturally, I'm speaking from a guy's point of view).

If the relationship was so bad in the first place that you had to leave it, what do you think has changed that makes you believe it won't be exactly like it was? Did she suddenly have an earth-shattering revelation that opened up her eyes and made her change her evil ways? OK, so maybe the sex was great, but do you seriously think you're only going to find great sex with one other human being on the planet? Human beings are sexual creatures! We like sex! And with millions of other human beings out there, you have to believe there's more than just one that you're capable of having GREAT sex with! Besides, do the math – the percentage of time you actually spend engaging in sex (great or not), versus the actual amount of time you spend putting up with the other person's bullshit (the same bullshit that made you crazy to begin with), makes *any* sex a moot point, doesn't it? Or perhaps you're just stuck in your tiny rowboat with one oar, and because your world is so small, you can't help but keep circling back to the same person? Or, maybe, just maybe, you simply are that desperate?

Whatever the reason – don't do it! Go west, my friend! There's a reason why you only hear about that *one* couple that was married, split up and then got back together. Truthfully, doesn't that couple (after they're back together) seem a little too happy, a little too Stepfordy (if you know what I mean), a little too, well... not right? That's because, and I don't care how many times they tell you over and over again (how and why) their "second time around" is the greatest thing since Caller ID, you should *never get back with an old girlfriend or wife.* It doesn't work!

The other day, my brother-in-law was telling me about his latest break up with his girlfriend. After he caught her cheating on him (for the second time!), he somehow managed to forgive her and ended up getting back together with her. Before I say anything in return, I allowed him to say his piece, thinking she must have him under some sort of magical spell that makes him powerless to break free! At the end of his whole "he said/she said" yarn, he finished by telling me, "You know, I'm really hoping this is the last time. But if it's not, well, maybe next time things will be different."

In my head, I'm thinking, *You know a lobotomy would probably do you a world of good! Or maybe, you can have a zipper surgically attached to your mouth, so this way you can stop yourself from telling too many people what's going on inside your head!*

"How long have you been seeing this woman?" I asked.

"Three years."

Three years! Forget the lobotomy! He needs a complete head transplant! His entire brain is just too far gone! He's the Tin Man! Get a can opener so we can pry this sucker off and rivet on a new head!

This whole conversation only served to remind me why my brother-in-law is in the exit-the-planet-line and he's not coming with the rest of us. *Bottom line, if you're not happy – get out!* But I also understand it's not my business to advise someone from another planet on matters of the opposite sex. So instead, I kept my mouth shut and listened to his insanity. But truthfully, here's what this whole situation boils down to – he's not the kind of guy who would *ever* read a book like this – or, if he did, understand it. To that point, I'm just going to stop myself right here and not take up any more space on this page. But damn it! If ever there was an example of someone who's going to be miserable the rest of his life all because he doesn't know the Golden Tidbit Rule – *Never get back with an old girlfriend or wife* – it's him. He would wear the crown, hoist the trophy and cash the check! Enough said!

167

Ted Danson and Bobby. "Cheers!"

Chapter 14
PARTING WORDS

First, thank you for allowing me to share my words. I hope they were entertaining. But beyond that, I hope my words were received in the spirit in which they were written.

Do I think I'm the next Hemingway? I may have developed hemorrhoids sitting and typing for such extended periods of time, which is sort of Hemingway-esque... and that's as close to being an actual writer as I'm ever going to get!

At the start of this book, I told you I undertook this journey along unfamiliar paths because of a challenge Jill tossed at me, "Well, if your 'words of wisdom' are so important, that special, that necessary, that wise... why then don't you just write them all down and put them into a book?"

I'm not sure if she said that because she knows I never back away from a challenge (if she'd added, "I double dare you," I would've started writing this book on my hand, right there in the car), or whether she said it just so I'd stop spouting out all my "life lessons" to our daughters. Either way, "Thank you, Jill, for continuing to know what's best for me, and for the love and support to see that I followed and implemented your wise words!"

Now that I've reached the end of this endeavor, it feels a lot like how I feel when I come down off the stage after a performance – I'm tired and energized at the same time! And just like after a performance, during some of the areas I covered, I could actually feel the audience (in this case, you, the reader) right there with me, our tuning forks in perfect harmony, and I knew that you knew exactly what I meant. In the same breath, do I think there are some areas that aren't as strong as others? I'd be lying if I said no. Because, of course, there are! Putting your thoughts and private beliefs down on paper is damned hard! But I did my best. I was truthful and honest, which is the most anyone can do.

But all and all, I'm proud (and relieved) that I accepted

169

Jill's challenge and hope that by reading this book you at least took away this:

We're all the same, and none of us are in this world for all that long. We must learn to love and respect each other and understand there is a greater power driving the bus. We're only passengers. Our job is to enjoy the ride!

THE END